simple soldering

A Beginner's Guide to Jewelry Making

Kate Ferrant Richbourg

INTERWEAVE
interweave.com

EDITOR
erica smith

TECHNICAL EDITOR
susan lewis

ART DIRECTOR
liz quan

PHOTOGRAPHER
joe coca

LAYOUT + DESIGN
pamela norman

PRODUCTION
katherine jackson

Interweave Press LLC
201 East Fourth Street
Loveland, CO 80537
interweave.com

Printed in China by Asia Pacific
Offset Ltd.

Library of Congress
Cataloging-in-Publication Data

Richbourg, Kate Ferrant.
 Simple soldering : a
beginner's guide to jewelry
making / Kate Ferrant
Richbourg.
    pages cm
 Includes index.
  ISBN 978-1-59668-550-5
 1. Jewelry making. 2. Solder
and soldering. I. Title.
 TT212.R53 2012
 745.594'2--dc23
                2012022405

10 9 8 7 6 5 4 3 2 1

contents

simple soldering

introduction

Welcome to the wonderful world of soldering and fabricating metal jewelry! If you are reading this book, you may currently be using beads as your main medium and are looking to take that next step into metalwork. Or perhaps you are just starting out in jewelry design. Sometimes as designers we just can't find prefabricated pieces that match the vision in our mind's eye. What's the solution? Make your own, of course!

Adding handcrafted metal elements to your jewelry allows you to start from the ground up and create pieces that are completely yours. Once you get the hang of forming, cutting, and soldering metal, the possibilities are nearly endless. You'll love the satisfaction that comes when someone exclaims about your beautiful jewelry and you're able to say, "I made it!"

I have learned from many years of teaching that people can be intimidated by that first step into the world of metalworking. Because heat (coming from a butane torch) is used, there's a common misunderstanding that crafting with metal requires a large setup and heavy-duty tools.

But take a deep breath: It's not as expensive or dangerous as it seems. A few simple tools, a guide to proper technique, and common sense are all you need. Anyone can do this, and I will show you how!

I have taught thousands of people how to successfully wield a torch and make metal jewelry. During that time, I have encountered just about every mistake a person can make, and made some of them myself. In this guide, I will lead you through the steps to do it the right way and how you how to analyze and fix anything that doesn't turn out as well as you had hoped. All you need to start is a little confidence and good sense, and you will be sawing, soldering, and forming in no time. I will be there in print and on the screen (in the accompanying DVD) to cheer you on in your success and coach you through the tough parts.

It may take you a little time and concentration, but the rewards are great! You can do this, and I am here to help. Let's get started!

DVD how to use this book

This book and the accompanying DVD are going to act as your guide, teacher, and troubleshooter to help you understand the fundamentals of metalworking. They are designed to build a foundation of solid techniques and classic designs that you can use as a springboard to create your own pieces and give your work a personal touch.

We start with an overview of what soldering is, how it works, and why. Then I will discuss the tools and materials that are used in the projects in this book. After that, you are going to hone your skills in a unique sampler section, in which you will create sixteen 1" (2.5 cm) square pieces of copper featuring every technique used to make the projects later in the book. This sampler section represents the heart and soul of my teaching method and will allow you to learn at your own pace and focus on the process rather than the result. One of the biggest barriers that I encounter in my classes is the fear students have of messing up. By learning techniques on the sampler you can feel free to make mistakes—and learn how to correct them. By the time that you complete the sampler, your skills will be perfected.

After working on the sampler section you will be able to move on to making projects. By then you can make use of all the techniques you have learned with the confidence of an expert. Where you go from there is up to you. You might entertain the thought of jumping into your own designs or coming up with creative variations on what you've learned. Wouldn't that be exciting?

WORKING YOUR WAY THROUGH THE SAMPLER & PROJECTS

It is important to make your sampler before jumping into the projects. The sampler builds important skills!

Also, note that the projects are presented in order from easiest to most difficult. Before you tackle any project, please read the instructions all the way through. If necessary, refer back to the samplers referenced in order to brush up on the techniques involved.

ICON KEY

 tip

Through my years of experience making jewelry, I have learned a lot of tricks through trial and error. These helpful tips are marked with the icon above.

 meet a new tool

Certain projects require more specialized or advanced tools. I will introduce these as they are needed throughout the book with the icon above.

 DVD **see it on DVD**

Techniques featured in the DVD are highlighted with the above icon, so you know where to go to see it done in live action!

① the **basics**

Throughout this book, I will be using many terms unique to metal jewelry crafting. For this reason, I have included this chapter to give you a basic understanding of the language of the craft, as well as how soldering actually works and how the types and grades of solder affect the process. Although I highly recommend that you read this chapter first, don't be nervous if you have a few questions. All these subjects will be discussed in more depth throughout the book, but the basic concepts in this chapter will stand you in good stead for what is to come. Think of it as Soldering 101.

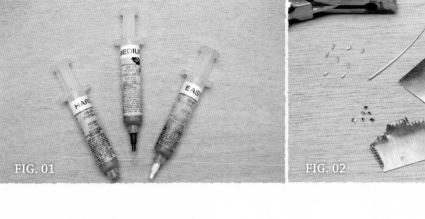

FIG. 01

FIG. 02

how soldering works

The solder in this book is silver solder, which is an alloy of silver and other metals (see Metals 101 at right). It is appropriate for the variety of metals used in this book. When placed on a metal surface and heated, solder will melt or "flow." As it does so, it will bind to any metal around it, provided that the metal is clean and the join is flush (completely touching). For this reason, throughout the book I have put many reminders about cleaning and filing your piece before soldering. As the solder cools, if it is touching two such surfaces, it will form a solid and sturdy metal bond, or join, between them.

Important: The solder is heated to the melting point by the surrounding metal more than the direct flame of your torch. The solder will not flow until the entire piece is heated equally. For this reason, it is important to heat the entire piece to be soldered, rather than just the solder join itself.

fire scale & flux

Most of the metals in this book, with the exception of fine silver, are alloys made with copper. When copper is heated with the torch, an oxidation of the metal occurs. The copper portion of the alloy reacts with the heat of the torch, and the oxygen in the air and forms a layer of black cupric oxide on the metal. The common term for this oxidation is fire scale.

The more astute among you may be asking yourselves, "If solder won't flow onto or bind to anything but clean metal, and fire scale forms as soon as you heat the metal, how does the solder flow at all?" That is an excellent question. In order to get the solder to work, there must be an extra ingredient, called flux, added to the solder. Flux retards the buildup of fire scale and allows the solder to flow and bind to the heated metal. Without the addition of flux, your solder will ball up on the surface of the metal and will not flow.

types of solder

PASTE SOLDER

Paste solder (**fig. 01**) is a ready-made combination of solder and flux. This type of solder is convenient for small soldering applications, such as jump rings, since it stays in place and is easy and quick to apply. It also works well with small components because the solder is sticky, which makes it easier to place pieces together. The down side is that it is more challenging to control where solder paste flows, so special attention must be paid to the amount applied and where it is positioned.

about flux

Flux comes in both liquid and paste forms and is applied to the surface of the metal using a natural bristle brush such as a paintbrush. I prefer using paste flux because it stays where you put it and thoroughly coats the metal surface.

METAL SOLDER

Metal solder comes in two forms: wire and sheet (**fig. 02**). A separate layer of paste or liquid flux must be applied to the surface of the metal. Small pieces of solder (also called paillons) are cut from the wire or sheet, then placed along the join in a precise manner. You will need to purchase the paste or liquid flux separately if you are using wire or sheet solder.

flow points & grades

The temperature at which the solder becomes molten is called the flow point. This is determined by the percentage of metals in the alloy. Solder is manufactured with different flow points for different purposes; these are known as grades of solder. When you purchase solder, the different grades are identified in two ways, either by the name or the temperature of the flow point.

✱ *Easy* (also known as soft) grade solder has the lowest flow point (1,325°F/719°C) and is used on pieces that have only one simple stress-free join, such as jump rings or on the last step of a multi-step piece.

✱ *Medium* (1,360°F/738°C) and *Hard* (1,450°F/788°C) grade solder are used when multiple steps of heating and cleaning are required or when the piece will have more wear and tear. Hard solder is best used for ring bands and connecting bezels, as it is the strongest solder and will endure repeated heating.

✱ Solder also comes in extra easy, which is used for simple solder operations such as pin backs or some jump rings.

It may also be worth noting that the color of the solder may be slightly different depending on its flow point, as this is determined by the amount of silver in the alloy. Solders that have higher flow points are more silver in color.

metals
101

For clarification, a pure metal is made of a single chemical element, such as **silver (Ag)** or **copper (Cu)**. An alloy is two or more pure metals melted together to achieve superior strength, color, or other desirable qualities.

There are other alloys of solder that come in brass and copper colors. I have chosen to use silver solder for this book for a couple of reasons.

First off, silver solder is the most readily available and comes in the variety of grades needed. (Grades are discussed above).

Also, silver solder is easy to see on the copper sampler tiles; therefore, it is easier to troubleshoot mistakes and note excess solder. If you do encounter a problem with excss solder, simply use a series of fine-cut files or fine-grit sandpaper to gently remove it. You will learn more about metals in Chapter 4 (see page 30).

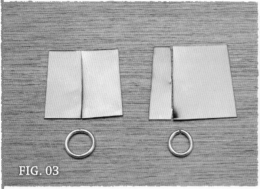

FIG. 03

FIG. 04

FIG. 05

steps for soldering

Regardless of the project, the steps for soldering are basically the same. I will, of course, be going through these in much more detail as you work on your sampler in Chapter 5, but here is an overview so you can know what to expect:

HAVE YOUR TOOLS READY

You should have everything you need in place before you turn on your torch. I strongly recommend reading all the instructions at least once before you begin.

DESIGN YOUR PIECE & FORM A PLAN

I will be doing this for you in the sampler chapter, but as you move into your own designs be aware that the order in which you do things will become very important. You will need to consider how many steps are involved and what grades and types of solder you will need to use.

CLEAN YOUR METAL COMPONENTS

Solder will not flow on dirty metal. The surface needs to be free of dirt, grease, and fingerprints. Clean all components to be soldered with a bleach-free cleanser or degreasing dish detergent and rinse thoroughly.

FIT THE PIECES TOGETHER

All components must fit tightly together. Any gaps or ill-fitting parts will result in a poor solder join or a piece that will not solder together at all (**fig. 03** illustrates a poorly fitting join [right] and a clean join [left]). You cannot fill a gap by packing solder into it. To fit the parts, file all edges and seams flush.

APPLY THE SOLDER

Once pieces are fitted and cleaned, it is time to position the piece on the soldering surface, add flux, if necessary, and then place the solder (**fig. 04**). Place just enough to complete the join. You will really get a feel for how much to use as you work through the sampler chapter.

BEGIN HEATING

This is the important step of bringing the surface of the metal up to temperature (**fig. 05**). Remember, it is the even heating of your piece that melts the solder, not the direct flame of the torch.

COMPLETE THE JOIN

When the entire piece starts to glow a bright orange (in dim light), that is the critical moment just before the solder will flow (**fig. 06**). You will quickly focus the flame on the join to

FIG. 06

FIG. 07

FIG. 08

coax the solder to a molten state. If the solder is exposed, you should see the solder suddenly become liquid and start to flow.

QUENCH

This is the process of cooling your metal. Use tweezers to pick up your piece and quench it in a metal quench cup full of water (**fig. 07**). Once you have done this, you can touch it with your hands.

REMOVE FIRE SCALE

As noted above, fire scale will form on the surface of your piece during heating. You will want to remove this before your next soldering step and again when your piece is finished to return the metal to the original color (**fig. 08**). To do this, you will use a citric acid–based cleaner or chemical pickle. This will be discussed more in Chapter 3.

next steps

Alrighty! Now that you have a basic understanding of what soldering is and how it works, let's go on to look at what you are going to need to get started. Don't be put off by what may seem like the long list of steps above. As we go through the sampler, you'll be learning these one at a time, and I will guide you every step of the way. By the time you start making the projects in the last chapter, you will be so comfortable that making jewelry will be a walk in the park!

soldering rules

* Your metal must be clean.
* Make sure your solder joins are flush.
* Heat the metal, not the solder.
* Your metal needs to be evenly heated.

2 setting up a **work space**

You were on your way to becoming a soldering genius from the moment that you picked up this book. Having the desire to make jewelry out of metal has already set you on your path. Now, let's turn that desire into a reality by setting up your work space.

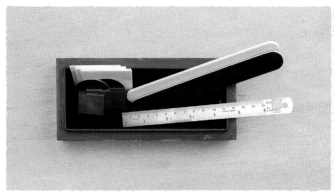

Start envisioning a space where you can work your metal. Do you already have a worktable where you create (perhaps it is covered with beads), or are you starting from scratch? Novice or expert, we all need a space where the creative muse can visit and stay a while. Whether you have a large room or a cozy corner in which to practice your craft, proudly proclaim it *My Studio*. That's the space where you can be creative, experiment, stumble, and succeed. Make it your own.

This book is designed to work in a small or shared space. I created all of the jewelry for this book in a space the size of your average closet—and not a big-fancy-house closet, either. What is important here is that you carve out a niche where your busy life can't intrude. The tools used in this book are portable, so you can tuck them out of sight when you need to reclaim your dining room table, if that's where you end up working. Look around and see where a small jewelry setup might fit. All you need is good light, a solid worktable, and adequate ventilation. There is no need to worry about what the professionals use. A few jewelry-making sessions spent sitting at your worktable will help you figure out what suits your needs.

get organized

Organization is an important step to successful soldering. Having all of your tools and materials within reach helps the process flow more efficiently and allows you to focus on the project at hand. I find that nothing kills my creativity faster than having to stop in the middle of a burst of inspiration to hunt up something that I need.

Start by dedicating a few bins on a shelf near your space to tools and supplies. If you don't have a permanent space set up, or if installing shelving isn't possible, you can achieve the same results with a few well-stocked toolboxes. They can be stored away when not in use and are easy to pull out when you are ready to work. Having everything together makes it easy to pick up and go if you are taking a class or creating jewelry with others.

FAMILIARITY BREEDS CONTENTMENT

Give a thought to your supplies and how often you use them. (The next chapter will give you an idea of the tools you will use most often.) These should sit in the most easily accessible area. Get in the habit of putting things away in the same spot so that your table stays neat.

It's easier said than done, I know, but soon your hand will automatically know where to reach out and grab what you need.

A FEW TIPS FOR ORGANIZATION

* *Store metal sheet in plastic bins or drawers.* Sort them by metal type if you have a larger stash. Write the gauge (discussed on page 31) on the sheets with a permanent marker so you won't have to stop and measure when you are working on a project. The marks will fade when the metal is heated or when it's swiped with a cotton ball soaked in rubbing alcohol.
* *Keep small metal parts and findings contained in plastic tackle boxes or pillboxes.* We all know that small pieces like to live on the floor. Make sure the tackle boxes are divided into sections and have tight-fitting lids.

* *Label everything.* Make it fancy with a labelmaker or keep it simple with masking tape and a marker. If a box or bin has a label on it, it's less likely to get messed up with random items.
* *Keep works in progress together.* The simple act of storing all parts for a project together in a plastic baggie makes it easy to pick up a project at a later date. I keep all of my work-in-progress baggies together in a good-sized box with a lid. All my bits and pieces are together so I can sort through and easily choose which project I want to work on.

STORAGE SOLUTIONS FOR WIRE

Another problem I often encounter is how to store wire. It always seems to jumble up together in a big mess. Here are a couple suggestions on how to tame it.

* First, never let the wire see your fear. That alone will keep those coils in line.
* Failing that, store individual coils in an accordion-style file folder from the office-supply store. Mark each one with the type and gauge.
* If you prefer, you can use plastic sheet protectors. Insert a piece of heavy cardstock into each one to make it stiff and write the type and gauge of wire on it. Slide each coil of wire in the protector and put them all in a binder. It will be easy to flip through and find the wire you need. Remember to store them right-side up so the wire doesn't fall out.

improvise your space

Even if you don't have the time and money to spend on containers for your tools and materials, chances are you have things around your home that would add interest and your own personal touch to your work space. Look around for items that you can use to hold your supplies. Vases, pitchers, jars, and small decorative boxes can be reincarnated as storage for your pieces and parts—plus, they

safety "musts"

* Use common sense.
* Don't use a torch or sharp tools if you are tired or frustrated. That's the time to take a break. Stop and walk away from your worktable, stretch, and breathe! Do a yoga pose. Dust the top of the refrigerator. Whatever you do, just taking a break in the action will help. You'll return to your worktable refreshed and refocused.
* Read all the labels and instructions that come with your tools and equipment. You might be surprised at what you learn. Remember, being prepared is half the battle.
* Don't use a torch without a fire extinguisher handy. Make sure that it is in good working order and that you know how to use it.
* Always wear safety glasses while cutting metal sheet and wire or using the torch. Not only are eyes the windows to the soul, but they are pretty important for making jewelry. Let's take care of them.
* Take care of your hands, too. Use rubber gloves when working with oxidizing solutions or other irritants.
* Work in a well-ventilated area. Healthy lungs are happy lungs.

WHETHER YOU HAVE A LARGE ROOM OR A COZY CORNER IN WHICH TO PRACTICE YOUR CRAFT, PROUDLY PROCLAIM IT *MY STUDIO.*

have the bonus of giving a unique look to your space. I found a computer table that I turned into a great worktable. For tool storage, I use everything from canning jars to coffee tins. I use a short metal file cabinet for my hammering and soldering surface.

You certainly can go fancy if you want, as there are a variety of ready-made tool racks and organizers that you can purchase to keep everything in its place, but you don't have to.

lighting & magnification

Good light is important when you are doing precise work, but dim light is needed while soldering. A portable task lamp is perfect for this purpose. It can be set close to your work area and turned off to make it easier to see the heated metal when soldering.

Since soldering requires the precise fitting of small pieces and components it stands to reason that you need to see what you are doing. If your eyes are just fine without any magnification, lucky you! But for those of us who do need reading glasses, you may find that you can't see as well as you need to do this fine work. Pick up an inexpensive pair of reading glasses at the drugstore that have a slightly higher magnification than your current pair. You'll be surprised at how much a little increase will help you see those small shiny objects. Getting a new pair of glasses is far easier than soldering at arm's length! Better glasses and good light will really contribute to your success.

safety

This is a serious subject, but there is no need to feel overwhelmed. Follow a few simple rules and you'll be soldering like a pro in no time.

FIREPROOFING

Sheet metal is the perfect material for fireproofing your surroundings. Many times it can be found in smaller sheets at your local hardware store. Or, if you have a sheet-metal supply company near you, it's pretty easy to have some cut for you. The edges will be sharp. Strips of duct tape folded around the edges of the sheet will take care of that. You will need about a 2' × 2' (61 × 61 cm) piece for your worktable and a 3' × 4' (91.5 × 122 cm) piece for the floor. These pieces will be fairly light and can be stored away when not in use. Place your solder setup (see page 20) on a cookie sheet with edges (sometimes called a jelly roll pan). The edges will prevent hot metal from rolling off and onto your lap or the floor. The pan should be large enough to hold your kiln brick, tweezers, quench bowl, and torch, but small enough to set out of the way when not in use. If you keep all your soldering tools on this pan when you put them away, you will always be able to find them when you need them.

So now that you are armed with a good strategy for organization, let's take a look at what tools and materials you need to make your jewelry.

3
the **tools**

I love tools! This section is an overview of the tools you will need to get started working with metal.

For the sake of convenience, I have organized this chapter into three tiers. The first, your "Solder Setup," will be essential to any project requiring soldering. The sections that follow outline basic tools according to their function. These tools are used in just about every project and sampler and should be at the top of your shopping list. Finally, in "Advanced Tools," I will be touching on some of the more specialized tools used to perform more specific tasks. These are only used for certain projects and samplers and will be discussed as we use them later on, but I have listed them here first to give you a brief overview.

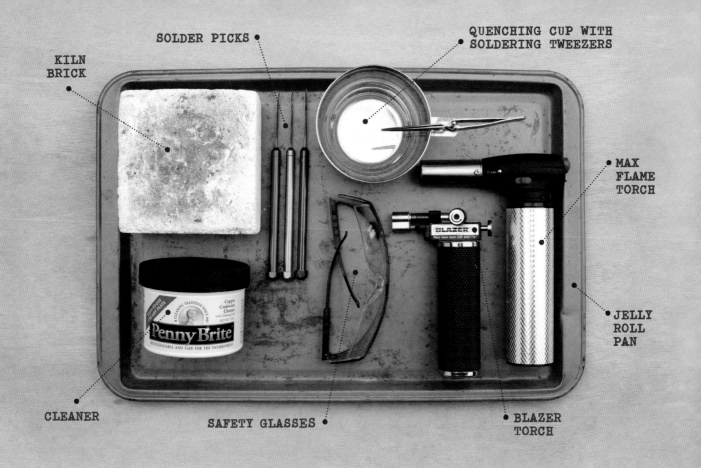

SOLDER PICKS

QUENCHING CUP WITH
SOLDERING TWEEZERS

KILN
BRICK

MAX
FLAME
TORCH

JELLY
ROLL
PAN

CLEANER

SAFETY GLASSES

BLAZER
TORCH

Here are the basics. These are the minimum tools you will need to start cutting, shaping, and soldering metal, so they should be your first priority.

DVD solder setup

This is the basic setup that you will need to solder one piece of metal to another. (You will, of course, also need solder, which is discussed on page 10, as well as in the sampler chapter.)

When you solder you will almost always use each of the tools in this group, so it's best to store them together. For the sake of simplicity, I will refer to this group as the "solder setup" in later chapters.

TORCH

All the projects in this book are designed to be soldered with a butane torch. A butane torch is portable, easy to use, and requires fuel that is readily available. I use two torches in this book that are specifically made for jewelry, the Blazer and the Max Flame. They both work the same way, but the major difference between the two is the size of the flame. Both of the torches heat up to 2,500°F (1,371°C), but the flame size makes them suitable for different projects.

✳ The *Blazer torch* has a finer, more tapered flame and is the torch of choice for smaller operations when a more concentrated form of heat is required. This includes making balled head pins, soldering jump rings, and fabricating projects that are 1" (2.5 cm) and smaller.

✳ The *Max Flame torch* has a larger flame that can cover more surface area and heat a larger piece quickly. Bigger pieces are better served by this torch.

KILN BRICK

The kiln brick is made of pumice stone and has a surface that can be carved to hold pieces on edge while soldering. It is perfect for beginners since it is inexpensive and durable. The surface absorbs the heat of the torch and reflects it back on to the piece being soldered, speeding up the heating process.

JELLY ROLL PAN

This one is pretty self-explanatory. You always want a nonflammable surface under your kiln brick, and the edges keep any wayward pieces of hot metal from going where they shouldn't.

SOLDER PICKS

Picks are used to place solder and to nudge pieces into position during soldering. Pick handles that come in different colors. Use one pick per solder grade so as not to cross-contaminate your solder. I use the blue for easy, yellow for medium, and red for hard. It doesn't really matter which you use for which, as long as it is always the same.

QUENCHING CUP

This is a metal bowl filled with water to cool the metal after pieces have been annealed or soldered. A specialty bowl for this purpose comes with soldering tweezers and has a stem to hold them. Be careful not to touch the metal with your hands between when it is heated and when it is quenched. (This may seem like a no-brainer, but anyone who's ever cooked in a kitchen knows it's easy to forget and accidentally grab hot metal.)

SOLDERING TWEEZERS

Also known as cross-locking tweezers, this tool grips objects tightly in its jaws. The object is released when the tweezers are squeezed. Tweezers are used to handle objects during soldering.

CLEANER

As mentioned in Chapter 1, each time you heat your metal, you will need to clean it afterward to remove fire scale and flux residue. There are a couple of products available for this purpose. I have used both of these methods for the projects in this book. You can use whichever suits your needs best.

Penny Brite is a brand of citric acid cleaner originally designed to clean copper cooking pots. I have discovered that it also removes fire scale very well. It has the advantage of being nontoxic and, unlike traditional pickle, does not require heating. This is why I recommend it to the beginning metal worker even though, in order to get the fire scale off, it does require a bit more elbow grease than pickle does. Also, note that Penny Brite has micro abrasives in it. So if you use it on silver, please do so carefully, or use pickle instead. I apply the Penny Brite with a damp toothbrush and give the piece a good scrubbing. Be sure to rinse the piece thoroughly under running water to remove any residue on the metal. When you are done, you just put the top back on the tub and stick it in the cupboard.

Pickle is made of sodium bisulphate granules that, when mixed with water and heated, form an acid solution. The advantage to using pickle is that it removes fire scale and flux residue quickly by simply submerging your piece—no scrubbing required! It also pentrates detailed areas more easily. However, pickle requires more equipment and safety measures than Penny Brite. (See page 22 for use and handling of pickle.)

(See page 22 for use and handling of pickle.)

kitchen torch vs jewelry torch

You already may have a butane torch that you use in your kitchen. (Crème brûlée, anyone?) If you are considering using your kitchen torch, make sure that it is mostly made out of metal. The torch is lit for an extended period of time during the jewelry-making process, and prolonged heat may cause plastic torches to melt. Torches that are mostly metal last a lot longer than plastic ones. You should also be aware that a kitchen torch does not have the same heat capacity or burn time as a torch that is made for jewelry. It may not get hot enough to solder larger pieces.

SAFETY GLASSES & FIRE EXTINGUISHER

Of course, you will also want to include safety glasses and a fire extinguisher with this setup. Safety is a good habit to get into. Make it a part of your setup process and you'll always be prepared.

bench & hammering tools

BENCH BLOCK

A bench block is a steel block with a polished metal surface. It supports metal for hammering, texturing, and stamping. Take care to keep the surface as smooth as possible. Any marks on the block will transfer to the metal during hammering.

CHASING HAMMER

You will need a hammer for forming and flattening metal. I find most hammers called "chasing hammers" work well for this purpose. Traditionally, chasing hammers are used to strike chasing tools to shape and work metal, but I prefer to use this hammer directly on the surface of my metal. Consequently, I never use the hammer to strike tools or stamps so the face remains unmarred. The head is slightly convex on one side and has a round ball on the other. I use the convex side to flatten and shape metal and the ball side to texture.

using sodium bisulphate pickle

Use a small Crock-Pot to prepare the pickle. Mix the pickle in the pot before you plug it in. To do this, pour in about ⅛ cup (30 ml) granular pickle and add 1 cup (.2 l) of water. I suggest mixing pickle in small batches. Smaller amounts heat faster and are easier to store and dispose of.

Stir with a plastic spoon or chopstick. All utensils that are used for the pickle should be reserved just for this purpose. You will also need a pair of copper or wooden tongs, because using steel tweezers will give the pickle a charge and cause any copper in the solution to plate onto the metal that is being cleaned.

Place the Crock-Pot on a metal cookie sheet or other protective surface and plug it in. Keep the lid on the Crock-Pot at all times to prevent fumes from getting in the air. Wear gloves and safety goggles whenever working with this chemical.

You will also need a bowl—I use an old half-pint–sized plastic food-storage container—near the pot for rinsing your metal pieces after they come out of the pickle. Fill this bowl with a mixture of about 2 tablespoons (28 g) baking soda and 1 cup (.2 l) water. The baking soda will neutralize the pickle once your piece is clean.

To clean your piece, simply drop it into the pickle pot and wait a minute or two for the fire scale to dissolve. Then take the piece out of the pot and place it in the rinse bowl. Remember to use copper or wooden tongs! Once the piece has been rinsed in the baking-soda solution, it is safe to touch. Dry it thoroughly before your next metalworking step. Remember to unplug the Crock-Pot when it's not in use.

To store, wait until it cools, then carefully pour the pickle solution into a glass jar with a tight-fitting lid. Mark this jar clearly as Jeweler's Pickle and store it with other hazardous household chemicals.

During use, the level in the pickle pot will reduce over time. As this happens I just add a bit more water and granules to keep the pickle strong. Gradually, your pickle will lose its effectiveness and become bright blue. At this point, mix a new batch. To do this, add baking soda to the pickle mixture slowly and carefully, one teaspoon at a time, because adding baking soda will cause the pickle to foam up. Once the pickle no longer foams when the soda is added, it is neutralized and may be disposed of. It still contains copper, however, and must be disposed of at a hazardous-waste facility.

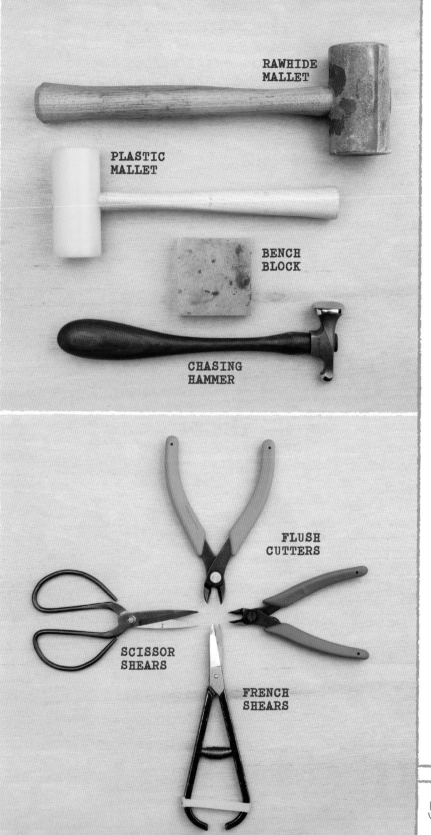

 damp it

If the noise of whacking away at those blanks is driving your neighbors or your family batty, I suggest placing a mouse pad from an office supply store under your bench block. It will dampen the sound quite a bit. You can also purchase a small leather sandbag for this purpose.

PLASTIC OR RAWHIDE MALLET

These are also known as soft-blow hammers. They are used for flattening and work-hardening (this will be discussed in Chapter 5). Hammering with either of them will not thin out or mark the surface of the metal.

DVD cutting tools

FRENCH OR SCISSOR SHEARS

French shears are used for making straight simple cuts in sheet metal. Look for shears with smooth blades. If the blades are serrated, they will transfer a serrated edge to the cut metal, which will have to be filed to make it smooth.

WIRE CUTTERS

The two most commonly used varieties of wire cutters are side cutters and flush cutters.

A side cutter has a slight dip where the blades meet. This type of cutter makes a "pinch" at the end of the wire when it cuts. The end of the wire must then be filed flush. The advantage of a side cutter is that the blades are usually thicker and therefore stronger.

Flush cutters cut the wire so that it is flush (flat) on one side. To use this tool correctly, turn the flat side of the cutter facing toward the end of the wire that you want to cut flush. Cutting with the other side leaves a pinched end that must either be cut or filed away. The blades on the flush cutters are thinner and sharper and can become dull if not properly cared for.

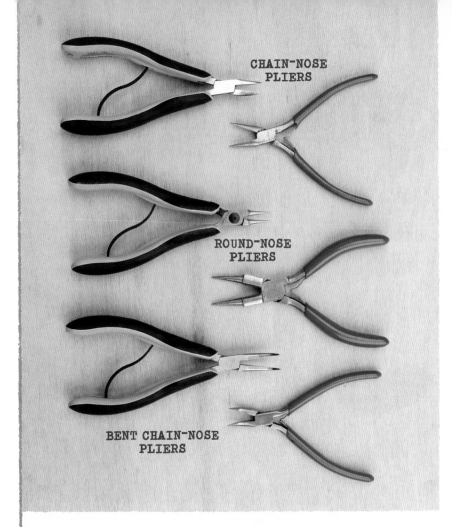

CHAIN-NOSE
PLIERS

ROUND-NOSE
PLIERS

BENT CHAIN-NOSE
PLIERS

pliers

CHAIN-NOSE PLIERS

Chain-nose pliers have straight tapered heads and are for gripping and bending wire and small pieces of metal. They should have smooth jaws so they don't mark the metal.

BENT CHAIN-NOSE PLIERS

Bent chain-nose pliers function like regular chain-nose but have a curved head as the name implies. They come in handy because they allow your hand to be at a perpendicular angle to your work. This angle makes it easier to open and close jump rings and tuck in wires when wrapping.

ROUND-NOSE PLIERS

Round-nose pliers are for looping wire. They come in a variety of sizes from small tips for fine-gauge wire to larger tips suitable for heavier gauges.

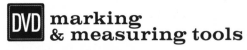

marking & measuring tools

METAL JEWELER'S RULER

A metal ruler comes in handy when marking metal. The thin metal edge allows for very precise marking. Try to find one marked with inches on one edge and millimeters on the other, marked in segments as small as ¹⁄₆₄" (.4 mm).

DIVIDER

The divider may conjure up images of those old compasses we used to draw circles in elementary school. It has two sharp points at the end of the legs that can be set a certain distance apart. I like to use it to mark lines opposite a straight edge by setting the distance and drawing one point along the edge of the metal so the other point inscribes a straight line opposite. You will use this tool quite a bit in the sampler chapter.

Wire cutter tips and suggestions:

* You should consider having several pairs of cutters, each suited to different gauges of wire. Pointed tip, fine-blade cutters should be reserved for soft wires that are 18-gauge and thinner. Heavier wires require a cutter with larger, sturdier heads.
* Avoid cutting at the tip of your wire cutters whenever possible, as that will prolong the life of the tool.
* Never cut hardened steel wire, including beading wire, using your good cutters. This may cause a permanent nick in the jaws of the tool. Find an old or inexpensive pair of cutters and reserve them for steel wire and other hard wires.

MILLIMETER GAUGE

This sliding gauge is used to measure the thickness of components and materials.

WIRE GAUGE

This is used to measure the thickness of wire and sheet metal with ease. (AWG is explained in more detail on page 31.)

PERMANENT MARKER

I use these all the time. They are helpful for annealing metal (the marks fade as metal heats and softens), temporary antiquing of stamped letters or designs, or just marking where you want to cut or punch a hole. Despite the name, these marks can be removed easily with a Pro Polish pad. I prefer the fine-tipped markers for more precise lines.

filing & polishing tools

HALF-ROUND FILE

The half-round file is perfect for filing the edges of sheet and the inside of ring bands. I use one that is 6" (15 cm) long and has a #4 cut (fine) surface.

NEEDLE FILES

Needle files come as a set with a variety of shapes. The round-needle file is perfect for enlarging holes in metal.

3M SPONGE SANDING PADS

Sanding pads are my go-to filing tools. They are flexible foam rubber pads that have micron-graded abrasives on the surface. Since they are flexible, they can mold around any shape for filing. They come in a set of five different grades. The coarser grades work well for sanding away rough spots, and the finer can be used to polish your designs. I prefer to cut them up in ½" (1.3 cm) to 1" (2.5 cm) strips for ease of use.

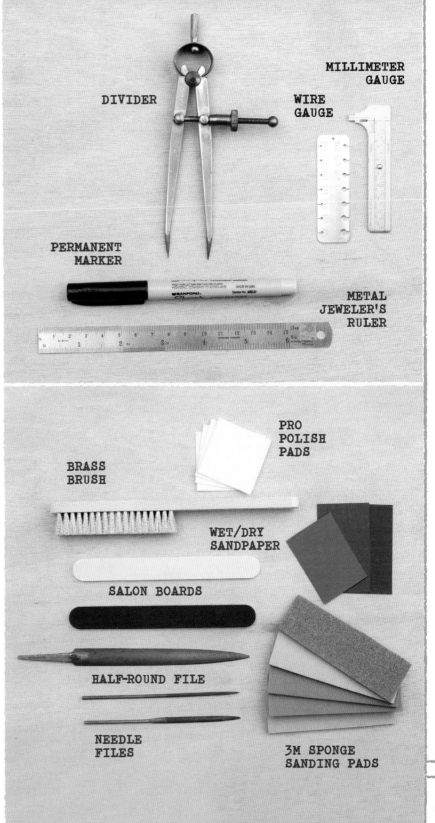

DIVIDER

MILLIMETER GAUGE

WIRE GAUGE

PERMANENT MARKER

METAL JEWELER'S RULER

BRASS BRUSH

PRO POLISH PADS

WET/DRY SANDPAPER

SALON BOARDS

HALF-ROUND FILE

NEEDLE FILES

3M SPONGE SANDING PADS

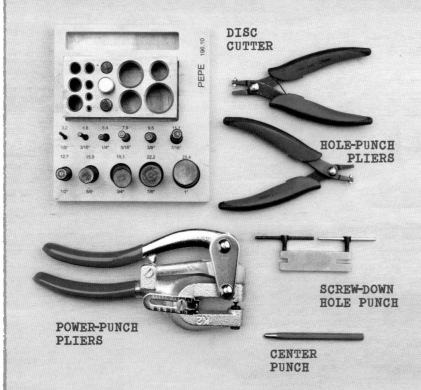

DISC
CUTTER

HOLE-PUNCH
PLIERS

POWER-PUNCH
PLIERS

SCREW-DOWN
HOLE PUNCH

CENTER
PUNCH

BRACELET-BENDING
PLIERS

TUBE-CUTTING
PLIERS

WRAP N' TAP PLIERS
(MEDIUM AND LARGE)

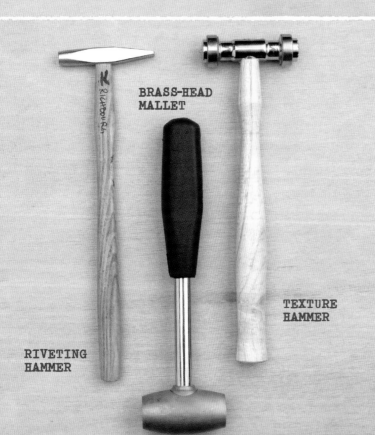

BRASS-HEAD
MALLET

TEXTURE
HAMMER

RIVETING
HAMMER

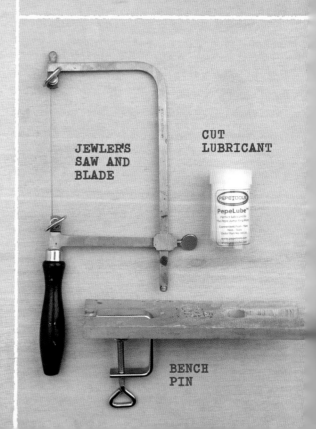

JEWLER'S
SAW AND
BLADE

CUT
LUBRICANT

BENCH
PIN

simple soldering

SALON BOARDS

Plain old salon boards like your manicurist uses are great multipurpose files. Go to the beauty-supply store and pick up a bunch. They come in a variety of grits and are great because they can be cut up into the perfect shape for filing. They are pliable, so they can bend around shapes and conform to the piece that is being filed.

WET/DRY SANDPAPER

This paper is found in automotive stores and in the paint section of many hardware stores—the higher the number, the finer the grit. A good mix to have is 400, 600, 800, and 1,200. The coarser grits are great for refining the edges of metal, and the finer grits work nicely to polish the surface.

PRO POLISH PADS

These 2" (5 cm) square foam-rubber pads have a micro abrasive surface that quickly polishes metal to a high shine. They remove oxidation and tarnish in a snap. Do not get these pads wet, or they will leave a film over the surface of your piece. Use until the pad has darkened on both sides.

BRASS BRUSH

I like using this soft-bristled brass brush to give a nice shine to my pieces. I run the brush under water, apply a small amount of liquid soap to the bristles, and give the piece a thorough scrub. Sometimes this gives my piece just the right amount of shine, and I can stop the polishing process there.

advanced tools

These are some more specialized and advanced tools that we will talk about more as we come to them in the sampler and project chapters. This section should give you a brief introduction, so you can see what they look like and learn a bit about their uses.

* **Hole-punch pliers** pop a hole into soft metal that is 20 gauge and thinner. (See sampler square 1, page 37.)
* **Power-punch pliers** punch holes in soft metals up to 16-gauge thick. (See sampler square 4, page 44.)
* A **center punch** is a metal punch that tapers to a fine tip. (See sampler square 4, page 44.)
* A **screw-down hole punch** can punch through soft metal up to 16 gauge. (See sampler square 12, page 63.)
* A **disc cutter** is a tool used to cut circles from sheet metal. (See Dapped Bead Caps, page 80.)

* **Tube-cutting pliers** hold a tube steady for sawing. (See sampler square 4, page 44.)
* **Bracelet-bending pliers** give a slight bow to metal and are used for bending a cuff shape. (See Monogram Chain Bracelet, page 134.)

* **Texture hammers** have a variety of patterns on the heads that mark metal when you strike it. (See Hook + Eye Clasp, page 80.)
* A **riveting hammer** has a thin narrowed face on one side of the head used to flare the rivet stem. The other face is flat to tap the formed rivet flush. (See sampler square 2, page 40.)
* A **brass-head mallet** is used for striking design stamps or other metal tools. (See sampler square 2, page 40.)

* **Jeweler's saw, blades, and cut lubricant** are for cutting metal. (See sampler square 3, page 42.)
* A **bench pin** is a flat strip of wood that clamps to your worktable, supporting your metal as you saw and file. (See sampler square 3, page 42.)

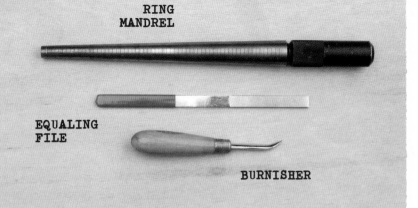

RING MANDREL

EQUALING FILE

BURNISHER

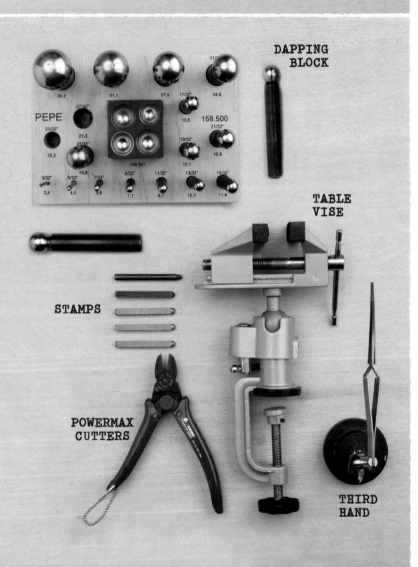

DAPPING BLOCK

PEPE

TABLE VISE

STAMPS

POWERMAX CUTTERS

THIRD HAND

* The **tumbler** is a motorized tool that consists of a rubber barrel mounted on a metal stand. To shine and finish jewelry, place the pieces in the barrel of the tumbler together with stainless steel shot, water, and a squirt of burnishing liquid (dishwashing liquid works well). The barrel is closed and placed on the stand to rotate. The tumbling action shines and work-hardens the piece. Be aware, though, that soft stones can be damaged in the tumbler; hard stones are fine.

* A **ring mandrel** works as a sizing tool and hammering surface for rings. (See Stacked Rings, page 84.)

* A **burnisher** allows you to apply pressure around the edge of a bezel or setting, bending the metal around the stone to hold it in place. (See sampler square 15, page 71.)

* An **equaling file** is useful for filing both ends of a ring band simultaneously to make them flush. (See Flower Ring, page 142.)

* A **dapping block** is used to curve metal circle blanks into domes. (See Sampler 14, page 69.)

* The **third hand** steadies objects for soldering. (See Sampler 13, page 66.)

* A **table vise** secures objects to keep them still while you work. (See Pearl and Silver 5-Stack Rings, page 102.)

* **Stamps** create words, phrases, and designs on jewelry. (See sampler square 2, page 40.)

* **PowerMax cutters** are useful for cutting heavy gauge and flat wire. (see Twining Vine Ring, page 118.)

So that's it as far as the tools go. If it seems overwhelming or prohibitively expensive, just check out one of the samplers or projects and get the tools you need to do that part. I have tried to arrange the samplers and projects from the simplest, which require the least tools, to the most complex. I have also provided a list of resources that sell jewelry-making tools and supplies on page 158 to get you started.

4 the materials

All right—so your work space is ready to go, you're all set up with tools, and you are eager to start soldering. But before you pick up the torch, let's take a closer look at the materials with which you will be working.

UNDERSTANDING YOUR METALS AND HOW THEY WORK WILL HELP YOU AVOID A LOT OF FRUSTRATION DOWN THE ROAD AND ALLOW YOU TO ACHIEVE BETTER RESULTS FASTER IN THE LONG RUN.

I know the last thing you want between you and the creation of that fabulous piece of art in your imagination is a science class, but trust me: Understanding your metals and how they work will help you avoid a lot of frustration down the road and allow you to achieve better results faster in the long run. So hang in there and don't skip this chapter!

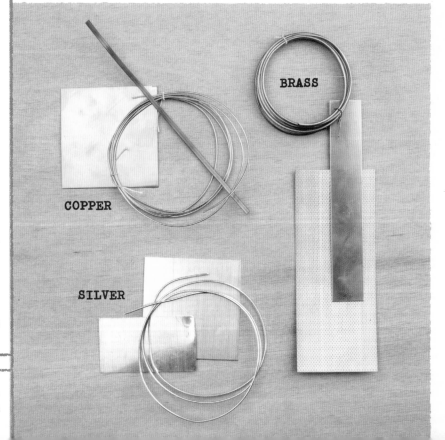

COPPER

BRASS

SILVER

metals

There are a variety of metals that are common to jewelry making such as fine silver, sterling silver, nickel, gold-filled, brass, and copper. They are classified under the term nonferrous, meaning these metals contain no iron.

I like to think of them as a family of cousins, slightly similar but each with its own personality. They heat at the about same rate and react similarly when soldered. Each is worked with the same methods and can be mixed together in the same piece. Mixing two different colors of metal makes an interesting design element in finished jewelry.

COPPER

Copper is a pure metal that is malleable and sturdy on its own, but is often alloyed with other metals to lend strength and work-ability. It is durable and takes oxidation and patinas easily. It does get heavy fire scale when soldered, but pickling and a little extra elbow grease in the polish stage restores the surface of this metal to a nice luster. Copper is very economical, and this makes it a great metal to practice on. The instructional samplers you will find later in the book all make use of copper.

FINE SILVER

Silver (also known as fine silver) is a pure metal. It must be made of at least 99 percent of the single element silver to be called fine silver. It is very soft and is mostly used in wire form for fusing. It can be soldered, but it is not used in fabricating as often as sterling silver because it doesn't hold its shape as well. In this book, we use it to make granules for decoration on our finished pieces.

STERLING SILVER

Sterling silver is an alloy of 92.5 percent silver and 7.5 percent copper. The copper in the sterling silver alloy adds hardness and work-ability to the silver and gives it some resistance

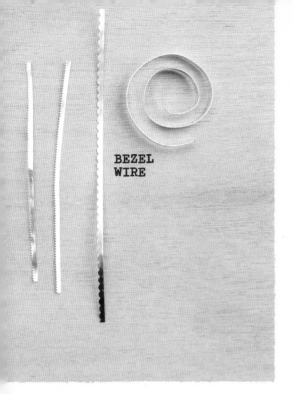

BEZEL
WIRE

so that it is not too soft to work with. The copper, however, makes this metal subject to fire scale and tarnish, unlike fine silver.

NICKEL SILVER

Nickel silver is an alloy of copper, zinc, and nickel. It is silver in appearance but does not actually contain any silver. It does not have the same shiny appearance as sterling or fine silver but has a nice antique look that is appropriate for designs with an antique flair. It also has the advantage of being much more economical.

BRASS

Brass is an alloy of copper and zinc. It has a rich gold color and works well for fabrication. Brass can be polished to a high shine and is a good choice when gold-colored metals are wanted in a design without the expense of gold or gold-filled.

GOLD-FILLED

Gold-filled is karat gold (usually 12 or 14k) that is mechanically bonded to a metal core. It is very

sturdy and will not flake off. It can be soldered; however, care must be taken when filing or cleaning so as not to remove the outer gold layer.

forms, gauges & uses of metals

All of these metals come in a variety of forms for fabrication. The thickness of sheet and the diameter of various types of wire are measured by gauge. Gauge is a standardized measurement that is applied to all metals known formally as the American Wire Gauge (AWG) scale. It all sounds very impressive, but all you have to know is the higher the number, the thinner the metal. For example, 18-gauge (.040" or 1.0 mm) is about the thickness of a dime, whereas 26-gauge (.016" or .40 mm) is much thinner—about the thickness of a postcard. This is a concept you should definitely note if you aren't familiar with it already. We're going to be talking about it quite a bit. Soon it will be like second nature, and you'll be chatting about gauge with ease!

When choosing the gauge of metal the form of the finished piece should be taken into account. Items that are going to have more wear and tear (such as ring bands) should be made out of thicker gauge. Items that have multiple layers or where weight is an issue (such as pendants or earrings) should be made out of thinner gauges. Different gauges of metals have standard uses.

* 16–18 gauge is used for ring bands
* 20–24 gauge is used for pendants
* 22–24 gauge is used for earrings, small charms, small component parts, and bails
* 26-gauge is used for bezels

SHEET

Sheet comes in a variety of gauges and can be hammered, textured, folded, and shaped. You can use shears or a jeweler's saw to cut strips or freeform shapes. A disc cutter is handy for cutting out circle blanks. You will learn how to do all these things later on in this book.

using a wire gauge

As noted in Chapter 2, you should try to keep your metals organized by gauge for easy access. If your wires get mixed up, a handy tool to have is a wire gauge (see page 25). This nifty tool has slots and measurements that help you determine the thickness of your metal with ease.

ROUND WIRE

Round wire is used for wrapping and linking beads together, shaping ear wires, and rivets. Heavier gauges can be used for making ring bands or bangles.

The hardness or temper of any wire is known as either dead-soft or half-hard. Dead-soft wire is just that, malleable and easily shaped. It must be work-hardened to retain that shape. (We'll get into work-hardening later in this book.) Half-hard wire is stiffer and more resistant to work with. It has more "bounce" when used for wrapping or making shapes and is often used for jump rings. I prefer to use dead-soft wire because it is easier to manipulate and handle. All the wire used in this book is dead-soft.

FLAT WIRE

Flat wire (also known as sizing wire) is measured in millimeters since it is measured by the width and depth of the wire. For example, "five millimeter by one millimeter flat wire" (5 × 1 mm) describes the dimensions of the cross section. Flat wire is usually stiff and should be annealed, or softened, before shaping. (Annealing will be covered in sampler square 5 on page 50.) This wire looks great when textured, or it can be left plain. It comes in a variety of widths and thicknesses. Flat wire works perfectly for ring bands or bangles. It needs to be cut with heavy-duty wire cutters or a jeweler's saw.

stones

Some of the projects in this book feature set stones (shown above). For these projects, I use cabochon stones. Cabochons are stones that are cut into a smooth dome with flat backs. They are perfect for beginners because it's easy to size and make a bezel for a cabochon.

BEZEL WIRE

This thin strip of wire is used for creating the rim of larger cups or bezels. Bezels are used for stone setting or filling with another medium, such as resin. (An example of a bezel project is the Flower Ring on page 140.) You probably want to get prefabricated bezel wire since most bezels require an exact fit, but you can also make your own in a pinch by cutting a strip off a 26-gauge sheet to the proper width for your bezel. We'll discuss how to do this in the Sampler chapter.

You can buy prefabricated bezel wire with decorative edges, such as serrated or scalloped, if that suits your fancy, but you might start out with the plain kind until you get the hang of working with it. You can find bezel wire in a variety of metals. For this book, I used fine silver bezel wire.

They come in a variety of shapes and sizes, but for the purpose of this book, we are going to stick to oval and round stones, which will make the setting process easier. Keep an eye out for other interesting flat-backed objects to set, such as buttons, coins, or vintage pieces. Anything that has a flat back may be set just like a cabochon and adds an interesting touch to your designs.

beads

Many of the projects in this book are meant to be mixed with beads (shown below). I love working with beads, and they make my finished pieces of jewelry all the more special when they include components that I have designed

and made. Clasps, metal beads, and pendants will all enhance your beaded creations and put a personal stamp on your designs. You can turn to your bead collection for inspiration. Sometimes just sifting through the assortment of shapes and colors will lend some ideas for your metalwork designs.

Okay. That's it! Thanks for hanging in there through the tools and materials chapters. I think you'll be glad you did. Now it's time to roll up your sleeves and get into some actual metalworking. This might be a good time to glance ahead and make sure you have all the tools and materials you need to get started on the next chapter. All set? Great! Let's go!

TOOLS

Metal jeweler's ruler

Permanent marker with a fine tip

French shears

Bench block

Plastic or rawhide mallet

Half-round file

Salon boards

Brass-wire brush

MATERIALS

You will also need a piece of 24-gauge copper sheet metal. A 4" × 4" (10 × 10 cm) piece of sheet metal will yield the sixteen squares required. However, since this is practice and you may need two (or maybe three) tiles for a couple of the more difficult projects, let me suggest cutting a 5" × 5" (12.5 × 12.5 cm) or even a 6" × 6" (15 × 15 cm) sheet so you will have ample extras. You may also want to have some Penny Brite or dishwashing liquid on hand for polishing.

5

creating your
sampler

Back in the old days, young girls would perfect their needle-arts skills by stitching a sampler. Completing a sampler honed their technique before they moved on to work on more complex pieces. That's how I want you to look at this section. These exercises are just stepping stones to the projects in this book. Instead of plying a needle and learning how to make perfect stitches, you are going to wield a torch and a hammer to shape 1" × 1" (2.5 × 2.5 cm) copper squares into samples of your skills.

You'll make mistakes here and there and that is fine. In fact, this section is where you will learn how to avoid or correct mistakes without worrying about damaging an important or expensive project! Goofs are a necessary and valuable part of the learning process. So don't worry if it isn't perfect the first time; copper is cheap. Take a break, try again, and you'll be a jewelry-making whiz in no time.

This sampler chapter uses sixteen copper 24-gauge squares, or tiles, each measuring 1" × 1" (2.5 × 2.5 cm) as base elements on which to learn and practice. In this initial section, we will go over the basic skills of measuring, cutting, and polishing used to prepare these tiles.

STEPS

MEASURE & MARK THE METAL

The first thing to tackle is measuring your metal sheet. Begin by marking the sheet into 1" (2.5 cm) sections. Use a fine-point permanent marker and straight edge to measure two opposite sides and make dots every inch along the edge. Connect the points by drawing lines with the straight edge.

You can also use your divider to measure straight lines. To do this, turn the screw on the tool until the points of the legs are open 1" (2.5 cm) wide. Measure the opening with a ruler from point to point. With the metal on a flat surface, place one leg of the divider against one edge of the sheet with the second leg resting on the metal surface. As you run the divider down the length of the sheet, the point on the surface will score a straight line in the metal. Cut the metal along the score, then mark the next line in the same way.

CUT THE METAL

Since these are fairly simple straight cuts, I find it easier to use my shears. They work just like a pair of scissors. You'll need to exert more force when cutting, but the idea is the same. Open the shears wide and place the metal toward the back of the blades, which is the most stable part of the tool. Cut the metal by squeezing the shears closed about halfway. Take short, straight "bites" of the metal with your shears all the way through. The cut piece will have a curled edge. Not to worry, this is easily fixed by placing the cut piece on a bench block and tapping with a plastic or rawhide mallet. You may also want to practice using your saw on some of these cuts, but we will get into that shortly (see page 42).

FILE YOUR PIECES

You will need to get in the habit of filing down your cut pieces. A piece of jewelry with rough edges not only looks unfinished but is uncomfortable to wear, so good filing techniques can make or break a piece. I begin by using a #4-cut half-round file as a first step to take down any rough edges and sharp points. Next, I continue to smooth the edges by using a series (two or three) of salon boards or sanding sponges from course to fine grit. Check the edges with your finger to make sure they are smooth.

Things to remember:
* Your half-round files work in one direction only, on the forward stroke. Release pressure when moving the file on the backstroke.
* Hold the file in the palm of your hand with your wrist rigid.
* The movement should come from moving your shoulder joint back and forth, not your elbow or wrist.
* Do not mash the file on the metal that you are working on. Use a light touch so that the file does not bind down into the metal, but instead glides smoothly.

POLISH THE SQUARES

My favorite first step in polishing is utilizing the magic of the brass brush. I think this is a wonderful tool for a quick polishing job.

To polish, run the brush under water and add a dollop of Penny Brite or a couple of drops of liquid soap. Scrub the surface of your metal with moderate pressure in a circular motion. Rinse your piece after 30 seconds of rubbing to check the shine. Repeat this process on the front and back of the tile until you are satisfied with the results. You can use this technique in lieu of or in addition to subsequent finishing steps such as tumbling or hand polishing with a

cutting tips

Be aware that if you are trying to straighten out your edge with the shears, you'll have tiny shards of metal that cut away from the edge. These little splinters are sharp! Keep a small jar with a lid next to you and drop the shards in there as they are cut.

Pro Polish pad. Remember that Pro Polish pads only work on dry metal.

THE FINISHED PRODUCT

You should now have at least sixteen 1" × 1" (2.5 × 2.5 cm) squares for making your sampler. Make sure these tiles are just the way you want them before you go on to the next step.

If you're not happy with the basic components, you probably won't like the finished piece. That being said, this is also a chance for you to experiment and discover how these techniques speak to you creatively. With that in mind, on to the first sampler piece!

troubleshooting

✳ Make sure to use a fine-tipped marker for measuring to get the most accurate cuts.

✳ Remember to use a plastic or rawhide mallet and a clean bench block on a solid surface to straighten out bent pieces. A few taps should do it, so you don't need to pound the heck out of it. Remember, you are work-hardening your tile with every hit.

✳ The brass brush works well when the piece is wet, but the Pro Polish pad can only be used when it is dry. Make sure you dry the copper between these steps.

✳ Be careful not to cut yourself on the sharp edges before they're filed down.

SAMPLER SQUARE 1
connecting metal using jump rings

This sampler will introduce you to the use of jump rings. You'll learn to make a perfectly flush ring that will stay closed, measure for the placement of holes, and create a loose join that will give your piece movement.

tools

Jeweler's ruler
Permanent marker
French shears
Bench block
Plastic or rawhide mallet
1.8 mm hole-punch pliers
Half-round files
Salon board
Medium Wrap n' Tap pliers
Flush cutters
Chain-nose pliers
Bent chain-nose pliers

materials

18-gauge copper wire. You will need about 6" (15 cm) to be able to wrap it. This will give you extra rings that you can use later.

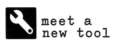

meet a new tool

hole-punch pliers

These handy tools pop a hole into soft metal that is 20 gauge and thinner. Piercing thicker metal may damage the tool, so use a different punch or a drill for heavier gauges. These come in a variety of punch sizes and have the advantage of being much quicker to use than a screw-down punch. The next sampler uses the 1.8 mm hole-punch pliers, but I will also be using 1.25 mm hole-punch pliers in later samplers.

wrap n' tap pliers

These are pliers with multi-stepped barrels that are used for shaping wire and sheet into curves and loops. They come in two sizes. The medium has barrel sizes 5 mm, 7 mm and 10 mm and the large has barrel sizes 13 mm, 16 mm and 20 mm. I use the medium-sized one for this sampler.

STEPS

CUT YOUR PIECES

1 Start by marking a line down the center of the tile (½" [1.3 cm] in from either edge) and cut it into two pieces as you did when making your squares (**fig. 01**).

2 File the cut edges smooth and flatten the pieces with your mallet and bench block as necessary.

3 Mark a set of three evenly spaced dots on one tile at least ¹⁄₁₆" (2 mm) in from the edge. Punch a hole on each dot using the 1.8 mm hole-punch pliers (**fig. 02**).

4 Use this piece as a template to mark the second set of holes by placing the punched piece on top of the other one and poking your marker through to mark the bottom piece. Punch the second half of the tile and set both pieces aside.

soften your punches

If you start by punching through a piece of cardstock or Pro Polish pad and leave it on the punch, it will act as a pad when you punch through your metal, protecting it from being marred by the pliers' jaws.

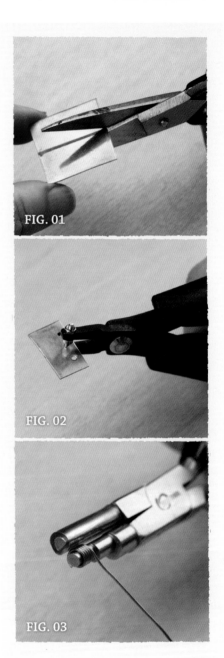

FIG. 01

FIG. 02

FIG. 03

MAKE A COIL

5 Grip the very tip of your 18-gauge wire in the jaws of the Wrap n' Tap pliers so it is against the smallest (5 mm) part of the coiling jaw. Hold tightly with the pliers and rotate the handles away from you for about a quarter turn to begin to form a loop. Open the jaws

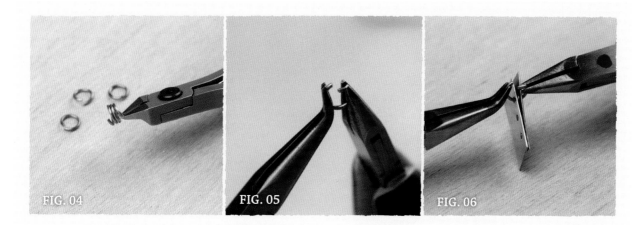

FIG. 04   FIG. 05   FIG. 06

and rotate the pliers back toward you, renewing the grip farther back along the wire. Use your free hand to guide the wire as it feeds into the tool. Repeat this process. With each twist and release, the wire should continue to bend around the jaw, making a 5 mm coil (**fig. 03**).

6 Be sure that the end of the wire you are holding in your free hand goes behind the emerging coil (closer to the pliers' handles) to give it room to grow.

CUT YOUR JUMP RINGS

7 When you have several rings in your coil, slide it off the end of the Wrap n' Tap. Position the head of the flush cutter with the flat side toward the coil and cut the exposed end of the wire flush. Flip the cutter so the flat side is facing away from the end that you just cut (**fig. 04**).

8 Clip the wire one layer down to make a ring that is flush on both ends. Check that the jump ring has two flush ends. There is now a pointed end on the coil where the ring was cut away. Clip that point off so it is flush as you did with the first cut and continue to flip the cutter with each cut to make two more jump rings.

ATTACH THE JUMP RINGS

9 Grip one side of a jump ring with your chain-nose pliers. Use your bent chain-nose pliers to grip the other side. Open the ring by pulling one side toward you and pushing the other side away, rotating the ends away from each other rather than spreading them so that the ring opens but keeps its round shape (**fig. 05**).

10 Slide both tile pieces on the ring through the matching holes. Close the ring securely by rotating it back until the flush ends meet with no space in between. Work the ring back and forth as you push it closed. The back and forth action will work harden the section of the ring opposite to the opening and help keep it closed (**fig. 06**).

11 Repeat for remaining rings.

troubleshooting

✳ Punch through a piece of cardstock to prevent your hole-punch pliers from marking your metal.

✳ Make sure the jump rings are completely flush on the ends. This will help them stay closed and will be necessary when you learn to solder them later.

✳ Always rotate your jump rings open using two sets of pliers. Don't spread the ends away from each other or they will become distorted and not stay closed.

substitute dowel for wrap n' tap

You can also use wooden or acrylic dowels for making your jump rings. Just wrap the wire around them in a tight coil and saw into the end of the dowel with your jeweler's saw (see page 42). Saw through the coil as you slide it off the dowel, forming rings. This is a good substitute in a pinch if you don't have a Wrap n' Tap.

SAMPLER SQUARE 2

texturing

Texturing is altering the surface of the metal. It provides an interesting contrast to smooth metal in a finished piece. This tile will teach you a few simple techniques for varying the texture of your pieces.

tools

Jeweler's ruler
Permanent marker
Bench block
A few letter or design stamps (including period stamp)
Brass-head hammer
Chasing hammer
Riveting hammer
Pro Polish pads

materials

One sampler tile

 meet a new tool

riveting hammer

This specially shaped hammer has a thin narrow head on one side, used to flare the rivet stem. The opposite flat side is used to tap the formed rivet head flush against the metal that is being riveted together to complete the join. We will get into riveting

later (see sampler square 4, page 44), but for this sampler, we will be using just the tapered end as a metal texturing tool.

brass-head mallet

This hammer comes in a 1 or 2 lb (.45 or .9 kg) weight. It is used for striking design stamps or other metal tools such as the punches used with the dapping block (see page 28) or the cutters used in the disc cutter (see page 26). The brass head prevents bounce back when the hammer is struck, which results in a solid and steady blow. The face of this hammer will become marred as it strikes the tools, which is fine, but you shouldn't use it directly on your jewelry metal, or it will transfer those marks to the surface of your piece.

stamps

Stamping provides an endless variety of possibilities to decorate the surface of your metal. There are numerous styles and sizes of letter fonts that can be used to stamp words, phrases, or your name on your jewelry. There is also a wide variety of design stamps for images, symbols, and general texturing. I used some letter stamps and a period stamp in the following sampler. The period stamp just makes a tiny indented dot that is great for texturing.

STEPS

DIVIDE THE TILE IN QUARTERS

1 Use a permanent marker and your jewelry ruler as before to make lines across your square, dividing it in quarters. You will be using one quarter for each technique and then polishing the lines away later (**fig. 01**).

STAMP A MONOGRAM, WORD, OR DESIGN

2 Choose the three initials of your name or stamp a word of your choice. Make sure your metal is on a bench block on a solid surface. Use your nondominant hand to hold

FIG. 01

FIG. 02

the stamp against the metal to keep it steady. I use my thumb on one side and all four fingers on the other side to get maximum control. If needed, rest your hand on the surface of the bench block. Strike the stamp with one swift blow of the brass-head hammer (**fig. 02**). *(Do not use the jewelry hammers that you use for shaping or forming, as the metal stamps will dent and damage them.)*

3 Design stamps are a little trickier to master than letter stamps. Depending on the complexity of the design, you may need to strike the stamp several times to get a complete imprint. Hold the stamp steady so multiple whacks do not result in a blurred imprint.

MAKE DOTS

4 In the next quarter of your tile, try playing with the period stamp. You can also use a center punch (see page 27) for this part. This is a great general patterning tool that I use quite a bit to add interest to my pieces. Striking the stamp harder will result in larger dots.

MAKE LINES

5 Starting in a fresh corner of your tile, use the tapered end of the riveting hammer to tap close-set lines across; then rotate the tile a quarter turn and tap another set of lines to overlap the first. In this way you can form a cross-hatch pattern.

MAKE DIMPLES

6 You can use the ball end of a chasing hammer to tap a close-set hammered pattern on the surface of the metal. Try it out on the fourth corner of the square.

REMOVE THE MARKER LINES

7 Polish the surface of your metal with a Pro Polish pad to remove the permanent marker. Voilá! You have four new techniques to add sparkle and interest to the surface of your pieces.

troubleshooting

✳ Always hammer and stamp on a steel bench block on a solid surface.

✳ Remember, you can use a mouse pad under your block to dampen the noise.

✳ Take the time to hold your stamps correctly and make sure they contact all the way around before you strike, especially for designs or larger stamps.

✳ Use the brass-head mallet on tools and not directly on your metal.

✳ The chasing hammer, on the other hand, should be reserved for hammering on your jewelry and never used on tools.

stamping tips

✳ If you are stamping your initials, it looks nice to have the last initial larger and in the center, with the first and middle initials slightly smaller to either side.

✳ You could mix up upper- and lowercase letters, if you do not have multiple-sized fonts.

✳ "Feel" the surface of the metal with the head of the stamp so that the design contacts the metal completely.

✳ Don't be afraid to get creative with your stamping. You can use a period stamp or center punch to stamp a decorative dot above and below your letters or further embellish the monogram using a simple decorative stamp such as a swirl or a spiral.

SAMPLER SQUARE 3

piercing & sawing lines in metal

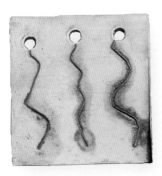

As you learned earlier, cutting metal is a basic necessity for fabricating jewelry. This step takes cutting metal one step further by teaching you to make a hole and saw a line into metal without starting from the edge.

tools

Jeweler's saw, 4/0 saw blades, and cut lubricant
Bench pin
1.8 mm hole-punch pliers
Wet/dry sandpaper
Permanent marker

materials

One sampler tile
Painter's tape
Paper and rubber cement (optional)

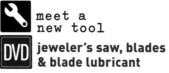

meet a new tool

DVD **jeweler's saw, blades & blade lubricant**

The jeweler's saw is made up of a metal frame with screw clamps on the top and bottom of the open side. There is also a screw clamp on the back of the frame that allows the mouth of the saw to be adjusted wider or narrower. The saw blade is a thin, flat piece of metal that has teeth on one side that face one direction. There is a space without teeth at each end of the blade.

You will also need beeswax or a synthetic cut lubricant to prevent your blade from binding as you saw through your metal.

bench pin

The bench pin is a flat strip of wood that clamps to your worktable. There is usually a slot cut out of the center. This allows you to place your metal on top so that it is supported for sawing and filing. The saw blade will run vertically through the slot as you cut, allowing you freedom of movement while keeping your piece supported.

what blade to use?

You can consult this table for an exact blade guide, but here's a great simple rule of thumb for choosing the correct size: About two teeth on the blade should be the same width as the thickness of the metal.

BLADE SIZE	TEETH PER INCH	METAL GAUGE
4/0	66.0	24
3/0	61.0	22
2/0	56.0	20–22
1/0	53.5	18–22
1	51.0	18–20
2	43.0	16–18

STEPS

MARK & PIERCE THE METAL

1 Cover the surface of the tile with painter's tape and draw some wavy or whimsical lines on the front. (I drew three.) These are the guides you will use to cut the metal.

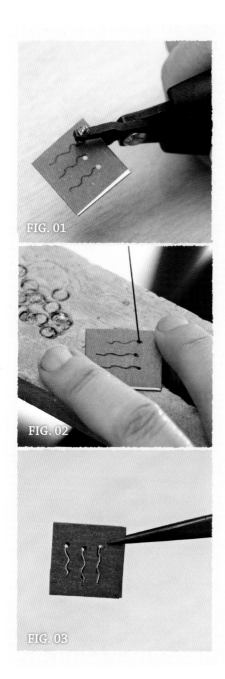

FIG. 01

FIG. 02

FIG. 03

Marks made on painter's tape will not rub off during sawing. Using your hole-punch pliers, pierce the metal at one end of each line (**fig. 01**).

PUT THE BLADE IN YOUR SAW

2 When saw frames are new, the jaws are sometimes pushed together so that the opening between them is narrow. You will need to loosen the thumbscrew on the back of the frame and extend the opening until it is slightly smaller than the saw blade. Tighten this screw to hold the frame open at this width.

3 Open both clamps on the saw frame and insert the un-serrated portion of the blade in the top clamp. Make sure to align the teeth pointing out and down (toward the handle).

4 Tighten the clamp firmly to grip the blade.

5 Prop the frame against your table and push it against the table's edge until the frame bows slightly.

6 Insert the other end of the blade into the bottom clamp and tighten. (For this sampler, you will want to put it through one of the holes in your tile first.) When you release the pressure the blade should be tightly tensioned in both clamps. Having tension on the blade is essential for sawing. If the blade is loose, it will bind and break.

7 Give the blade a pluck with your finger after it is inserted in the frame. If the tension is good, you should hear a high plink, like a note from a guitar string.

8 When the saw is not in use, prevent the blade from breaking by releasing one end from the frame.

SAW LINES

9 Following the instructions above, attach the blade to one side of your saw frame, pass it through one of the holes in your tile, then secure it to the other side of the frame. The tile should now be strung on the saw blade. Lubricate the blade by rubbing both sides over your beeswax or cut lubricant and set the tile on the bench pin so it is supported and the

sawing tips

✳ You don't need to apply a lot of muscle to cut with the saw. Pushed too hard, the blade will bind into the metal, and you'll be stuck.

✳ The saw cuts on the down stroke (pulling toward you). Apply more pressure as you pull it toward you and release as you push it back up.

✳ If the blade breaks or if you encounter binding or resistance, don't let it get you down. Sawing takes practice, and the good news is that blades are cheap. Just replace the blade and try again.

✳ If sawing directly on metal without the tape, you can also add the lubricant to the surface of the metal. It will adhere better and allow for smoother sawing.

✳ You can saw lines into a sheet to mimic a line drawing. Just make sure that the lines do not meet or the interior of the tile will fall out.

✳ You may also want to saw an interior shape out of a piece of metal to form an interesting washer or silhouette.

saw blade is able to move through the slot in the bench pin. Saw along the curved line to the end of the mark. You may find it easier to maneuver the saw if the blade is perpendicular to the metal (**fig. 02,** page 43).

10 Unscrew the blade and remove the tile. Repeat for each line (**fig. 03,** page 43).

11 Peel the painter's tape away after sawing the lines.

FILING THE LINES

12 Insert a very small piece of folded fine-grit sandpaper into each cut line and smooth the interior of the cut. Alternatively, a spin in a tumbler for 30 minutes will also smooth out the lines.

troubleshooting

✳ Before you start your cut, lubricate the blade on each side with a blade conditioner or beeswax so that the blade will easily saw through the metal without catching or binding.

✳ Make sure the blade is taut, the teeth are pointing the right direction, and you are not applying too much pressure on the saw.

✳ Sawing may take a little practice. Don't worry if a blade breaks. Just replace it and try again.

✳ As an alternative to the painter's tape method, you can also draw out a design, photocopy it, cut it out, and use rubber cement to glue it to the metal surface. Let the glue dry, then pierce and saw as above. Peel the paper away when finished.

SAMPLER SQUARE 4
DVD riveting

Riveting is an excellent way to connect metal. Having a solid knowledge of riveting is an important skill that every metalsmith should know. Different kinds of rivets can be made with or without soldering, and in this sampler, we will be making both kinds. It's a great decorative join and comes in handy, especially if you need to connect something that can't be soldered, such as a glass bead. This is also the first time you will be using your solder setup, so make sure you have all your tools and safety measures (see page 19) before you get started on this sampler. As always, I recommend that you read the entire soldering section before you actually do it.

tools

Power-punch pliers
Needle files
Permanent marker
Tube-cutting pliers
Jeweler's saw, 4/0
    saw blades,
    and cut lubricant
Bench block
Center punch
Brass-head hammer
Riveting hammer
1.25 mm hole-punch
    pliers
Flush cutter
Chasing hammer

Solder setup
Pro Polish pad

materials

One sampler tile
³/₃₂" (1.5 mm)
    diameter rivet tube
16-gauge sterling or
    copper wire
24-gauge sterling
    silver ½" (1.3 cm)
    diameter circle
    blank
16-gauge fine silver
    wire

meet a new tool

power-punch pliers

This tool includes seven different punches that range in size from 2.38 mm to 7.14 mm. It works on nonferrous metals up to 16-gauge thick. The small metal discs from the punched out holes make great components that can be textured and soldered onto your designs!

tube-cutting pliers

This tool holds the tube steady for sawing. The tube is gripped in the jaws of the pliers. Then a jeweler's saw is inserted in the groove to guide the blade as it saws through the tube.

center punch

The center punch is simply a metal punch that tapers to a fine tip. It can be used to texture in the same way as the period stamp or, as seen here, to flare tube rivets.

DVD working with your torch

In this sampler, we are going to start using the torch to heat metal. There are a few things you should know before you get all fired up, so to speak.

HOW TO FILL YOUR TORCH

Torches are sold and shipped without fuel, so you will need to fuel it up with butane before you can begin to solder. To fill the torch:

* Locate the valve on the bottom.
* Insert the tip of the butane canister (which can be purchased at most hardware and drug stores) into the valve on the torch and press down to dispense the fuel.
* The torch is full when the butane sputters around the valve.
* Always fill your torch in a well-ventilated area and wait at least one minute to let the gas settle before turning it on.

TURN ON YOUR TORCH & ADJUST THE FLAME

* Be sure to read all the safety instructions in the first section of this book (see page 17), as well as those that come with your torch before filling it or turning it on.
* You will want to make sure that you are in position and your flame is pointed toward your piece (and your nonflammable surface) before you turn on your torch.
* Make sure your quenching cup is at hand and has water in it, ready to cool your metal.
* Locate the switch or dial that starts the butane flow. You should hear a low hiss when you activate it. Then just press the ignition button.
* Some torches have a safety switch that must be depressed before the torch can be ignited.
* To turn it off, stop the butane flow with the same lever or valve you used to start it.

tube rivet

Rivet tube is specially made so there is no seam. This means it will not split when flared. It comes in many materials: copper, sterling, anodized aluminum. I used sterling for this project, but copper works just as well. Please note: aluminum tube should never be used on a piece where soldering or heating is required. It will melt and may be toxic!

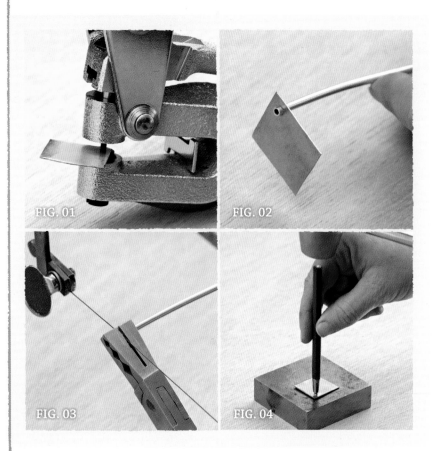

FIG. 01

FIG. 02

FIG. 03

FIG. 04

tip

Save the piece you punched out of the hole for use later if you like. (I used it in sampler square 12; see page 63.) Tiny pieces like this make great embellishments to add interest to your jewelry, so you might want to have a container with a lid set aside to keep them safe and available.

PREPARE THE RIVET

1 Use power-punch pliers fitted with the ³⁄₃₂" punch. Punch a hole in one corner of the tile about ⅛" (3 mm) from the edge (**fig. 01**).

2 Insert the rivet tube into the hole with about 1.5 mm protruding from one side (**fig. 02**).

3 The tube should fit snugly. Use a small round file to enlarge the hole if needed. Mark the opposite side of the tube at 1.5 mm with your permanent marker. The length of the tube should be about 3 mm from the end to the mark.

CUT THE RIVET

4 Grip the rivet tube with the tube-cutting pliers so the mark on the tube lines up with the groove in the jaws of the pliers. Put

the blade in your jeweler's saw and apply cut lubricant (see page 43). Hold the pliers with the tube steady in your off hand and place the blade of the saw into the groove in the jaws of the pliers (**fig. 03**).

5 Cut through the tube. If you have lined it up right, you should have a straight cut through the tube right were your mark was, giving you a 3 mm piece for the rivet.

RIVET THE TUBE IN PLACE

6 Insert and center the cut piece of tube into the hole and place the tile on your bench block so one end of the tube is sticking up. Place the tip of the center punch into the end of the tube. Tap the top of the center punch gently three times with a 1 lb (.45 kg) brass-head mallet to flare the edge of the rivet (**fig. 04**).

7 Flip the piece over and repeat on the other end of the tube. Repeat the flaring process one more time on each side and then use the flat end of a riveting hammer to give a final finish to both sides of the rivet by flattening it flush.

wire rivet
PREPARE THE RIVET

8 Using 1.25 mm hole-punch pliers, punch a hole in the center of the tile and another hole in the center of a ½" (1.3 cm) diameter 24-gauge sterling silver circle (**fig. 05**).

9 Stack the circle blank on top of the tile, lining up the holes. Use a round needle file to enlarge the holes slightly to accommodate the wire. Use your flush cutter to cut a piece of 16-gauge copper or sterling silver wire. Insert this through the holes in the circle and the tile (**fig. 06**).

10 Cut the other side of the wire flush, leaving about 1.5 mm on each side of the hole.

tube-rivet troubleshooting

✱ The amount of metal that sticks up from the hole relates to how large the rim is after the tube has been riveted. Depending on the gauge of your sheet, 3–4 mm is a good general measurement for a tube rivet.

✱ If the rivet is too long, the edges will split when flattened. If this happens, carefully clip the rivet away on one side using wire cutters and gently tug on the other with chain-nose pliers to remove the rivet and give it another try.

✱ Tapping the rivet too hard may split the rivet. Make sure not to over hammer the first side of the rivet. If it is hammered too much, it will be uneven on the second side. You want to coax it to flare gradually, one side at a time.

wire-rivet troubleshooting

✱ Make sure your flush cutter is right-side up so the cut end of the wire is flat and not pinched. A flat wire will rivet much better than a pinched end.

✱ If the holes that were punched in the metal pieces prevent the pieces from lying together tightly, gently tap them flat on a bench block using a chasing hammer.

✱ If the holes are too small, use a round file to slightly enlarge the hole to accommodate the wire. For best results, the wire must fit tightly into the holes and not wiggle around.

✱ If your wire is cut too long, it will bend over, rather than flare. If this happens, cut away a bit of the length from the end and try tapping out the end again.

RIVET THE WIRE & CIRCLE BLANK IN PLACE

11 Place the tile, circle, and wire from the previous step on your bench block (**fig. 07**).

12 Use the tapered side of the riveting hammer to gently flare the rivet wire by tapping across the top of the wire vertically and horizontally in a cross-shaped pattern. This will coax the metal in all directions, like rolling out a tiny piecrust (**fig. 08**).

13 After the wire has flared over the edge of the hole, turn the piece over and repeat on the other side. Continue turning and tapping about three times per side or until the

FIG. 05

FIG. 06

FIG. 07

FIG. 08

FIG. 09

17 Heat the bottom portion of the wire.

18 When the wire starts to glow, rotate the torch so that the flame lines up with the wire and is directly heating the end (**fig. 10**).

19 Concentrate the sweet spot of the torch (just in front of the bright blue cone) on the tip of the wire. You'll see the end start to glow, then become molten and shiny. That is the moment that the ball will start to form on the end. Flick the tip of the torch up the length of the wire to coax the ball upward. Remember that the molten metal will follow the flame (**fig. 11**).

20 Remove heat as soon as the ball measures about 2 mm and quench. Ta-da! This is the ball rivet.

A ball rivet can be made with 24- to 14-gauge wire. Thinner wire balls up really quickly and thicker wire takes more time. You may wish to experiment with a variety of wire gauges and sizes of ball ends. Fine silver wire makes the best ball rivets as the pure metal melts easily and results in a nice, smooth ball. If you experiment with sterling silver or copper wire, dip the tip in flux before heating. This will prevent fire scale and help the ball to form more smoothly. If you do use copper or sterling wire, you may need to clean it (see page 21).

rivet head has noticeably spread. As with the tube rivet, you don't need to tap very hard. To finish, tap the rivet flush to the surface of the metal on both sides using the large side of the riveting hammer.

ball rivet

PREPARE THE HOLE & WIRE

14 Use your 1.25 mm hole-punch pliers to punch the tile as above. Enlarge the hole with a round file if necessary. Cut 1½" (3.8 cm) of 16-gauge fine silver wire (not sterling) with your flush cutter. The wire should sit tightly in the hole. Set the tile aside for now (**fig. 09**).

FORM A BALL RIVET

15 Position the wire in your soldering tweezers so that it is perpendicular to the tweezers. Tilt it so that the wire is at a slight angle between vertical and horizontal and the bottom end is over your quenching cup. (You have water in the quenching cup, right?)

16 The secret to drawing a ball on the end of a wire is how you position the wire and the torch in relation to each other. Light the torch (see page 45) and hold it so the flame is perpendicular to the wire.

positioning your flame

If you look at the flame of the torch, you will see that it is a thin, blue, concentrated cone that emits a soft hissing sound. If the flame is bushy or slightly orange, that means that the flame needs to be adjusted. Many torches have a little collar on the head of the torch near the gas dial. This collar has a hole in it that should match up with a hole in the head of the torch. This controls the amount of oxygen that mixes with the butane gas. A slight rotation of the collar will line up the holes and sharpen the flame into a tight taper. This is the hottest flame, and the hottest point is just in front of the dark blue inner cone. This is known as the sweet spot. If the torch does not have a rotating collar, the flame should automatically adjust.

RIVET THE BALL IN PLACE

21 Place the ball rivet in the hole in your tile, ball side to the front of the piece (**fig. 12**).

22 Use a flush cutter to cut the excess wire leaving 1.5 mm of wire sticking up through the hole on the back side of the piece.

ball-rivet troubleshooting

✳ Make sure to read all the instructions carefully before using your torch.

✳ You may need to adjust your flame to sharpen the sweet spot.

✳ Start with the flame perpendicular to the wire. When the wire starts to glow, immediately move it to point right at the end. When the wire gets shiny and melts, flick the flame up the wire briefly, remove the heat, and quench. Remember, liquid metal flows toward the heat.

✳ Use a Pro Polish pad as a cushion on your bench block so your ball doesn't flatten too much as you rivet the back side.

✳ Fine silver is the easiest to ball and will not get fire scale.

✳ The finer the wire, the faster it will form a ball.

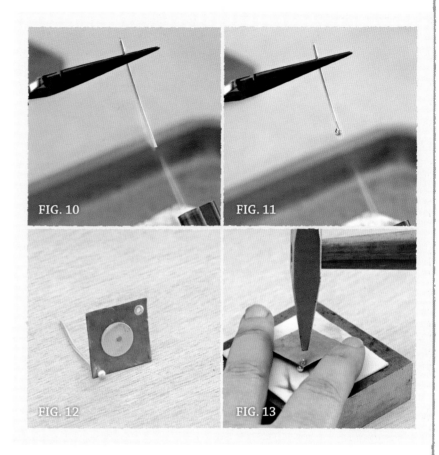

FIG. 10

FIG. 11

FIG. 12

FIG. 13

23 Cushion the surface of a bench block by placing an old Pro Polish pad on the surface. Lay the piece ball-side down on the pad. Use the tapered end of the riveting hammer to gently tap the end of the wire in a cross pattern as before until the wire has spread (**fig. 13**).

Finish with the large side of the rivet hammer as before until it is flush with the metal sheet. The rivet should be secure and not move. The ball will be flattened slightly, but should be intact on the other side.

SAMPLER SQUARE 5

work-hardening, annealing & cleaning fire scale

All metals have an atomic structure that makes them malleable. That means that metal can be shaped through hammering and bending. However, as these metals are repeatedly moved and shaped the crystalline structure of the atoms are moved out of alignment. The metal then becomes more brittle and harder to bend or flatten. This process is called work-hardening.

As you may imagine, work-hardening is a desirable quality in a finished piece that you want to maintain its shape as you wear it, but can be very frustrating if you are still forming and shaping the metal. I'm sure those of you with any metalworking experience have encountered this situation. That piece that seemed so cooperative when you were first shaping it just won't bend to your will anymore!

To solve this problem, you need to use a process called annealing. Annealing is making metal soft again through the application of steady heat. The atoms in the metal are brought back into alignment, restoring its workability.

tools

Bench block
Chasing hammer
Permanent marker
Solder setup
Pro Polish pad

STEPS

WORK-HARDEN YOUR TILE

1 Place the tile on the bench block and use a chasing hammer to lightly tap it. The strikes should leave no marks; you are simply compressing the metal together, not texturing. Though texturing also work-hardens metal. Check out that textured sample you made (see page 40)—stiff, huh?

2 Tap the entire tile until the piece has hardened. Note how hammering on soft metal will make a sound like a thud. As the metal starts to work-harden the hammering sound will sound more like a ping. This sound means it's time to anneal. You can anneal as many times as needed during the forming process, so don't be shy about it. Working with stiff metal can be frustrating and tiring, and life's too short for that kind of nonsense. Annealed metal will move much more easily and produce better results.

ANNEAL YOUR TILE

3 Start by making a heavy mark across the tile using the permanent marker (**fig. 01**). This mark will fade when the metal reaches annealing temperature, letting you know that your metal is heated sufficiently.

4 Place the tile on your kiln brick. Turn on the torch and begin to slowly sweep it over the metal, gradually heating the piece. Move the torch across the entire surface of the metal so it heats evenly. After about 30 to 45 seconds the metal will begin to glow a dull red. Maintain this temperature for about another minute. The permanent marker should fade around this time (**fig. 02**).

5 Heat for another 20 to 30 seconds after the mark fades. Turn off the torch and let the metal cool for a few moments. Carefully pick up the metal with the soldering tweezers and quench. The immediate quenching action aids the annealing process.

REMOVE FIRE SCALE

6 You will notice that your metal changes color and darkens in a way that the fine silver wire in the last sample did not. This darkening is fire scale. Fire scale will need to be removed to have a clean surface for soldering, but if you are just going to shape or hammer your metal some more and then re-anneal, you may not want to bother with this step until you have finished practicing on this tile.

7 To remove the fire scale using Penny Brite, open the jar and dampen the included sponge. Use the sponge to scrub a small amount of the paste over half the surface of your piece. Rinse and see how shiny it is in comparison to the other side! No more fire scale. (This is the method I recommend for those starting out because it is safer and more cost-effective, but you can also use a liquid acid

FIG. 01

FIG. 02

solution called pickle, which is discussed in-depth on page 22.)

fun with fire scale

You will notice that the fire scale takes on different colors at different temperatures. You also have the option of leaving it on as a colorful patina. Try just polishing the side of your sample where you left the fire scale on with a Pro Polish pad. Polishing will not remove the fire scale but will simply shine the surface. (You can also use a tumbler for this step if you have one.)

SAMPLER SQUARE 6

DVD flowing paste solder

tools

Solder setup

materials

One sampler tile
Hard, medium, and
  easy paste solder
Liquid dish soap

In the next three samples, you'll get comfortable using solder by observing how it melts and flows. You'll compare paste, wire, and sheet solder and learn the characteristics of each. By applying varying amounts of solder in different grades you'll get the hang of how much solder you will need when you make your finished pieces.

I find that paste solder is great for the beginner, as the solder and flux are combined in it. It is easy to place on your metal, and it stays where you put it. As you become more comfortable with using solder and are fabricating more complex pieces, wire and sheet solder may better suit your needs. They give you much more control over placement and a more precisely finished join.

STEPS

PREPARE YOUR TILE

1 Solder will not flow on dirty metal. The surface needs to be free of dirt, grease, and fingerprints. Clean all components to be soldered with degreasing dish detergent and rinse thoroughly.

APPLY THE SOLDER

2 Paste solder comes in a syringe with an optional tip that has a very fine point. I rarely use this tip as I feel that I have more control over where I place the solder when I apply it with a pick. To apply paste solder, remove the cap and extrude a small amount of solder from the syringe. Use the tip of the pick to lift off and apply what you need. Each amount of paste solder on the tip of your pick should be about the size of a 3mm bead and placed about ¼" (6 mm) apart depending on the size of the piece to be soldered. Begin this sample by applying a single 3 mm bead of hard paste solder in the upper right-hand corner of the tile (**fig. 01**).

BEGIN HEATING

3 Dim the lights in your soldering area so that you can see when the metal starts to glow in the next step. You don't want to have to stop and do this while heating. Turn on your butane torch as in the previous sample. Begin heating by circling around the outside of your tile while holding your torch about six to eight inches from your soldering surface. This will start gradually heating the piece of metal.

4 What you will observe as the metal heats:

✱ First, you will see the binder in the solder paste start to sizzle and smoke, then catch on fire. (Don't worry, that's supposed to happen!)

✱ Next, the surface of the copper will start to become discolored as the torch passes over it as it did when annealing. This is the fire scale forming.

✱ Finally, you should start to see the entire piece start to glow a dull orange. This means you're ready to move to the next step.

COMPLETE THE FLOW

5 Once your piece starts to glow, bring your torch closer and focus on the solder itself. You will see it melt and become shiny like liquid mercury. Observe how the liquid solder follows the flame as it moves (**fig. 02**). Becoming comfortable with this concept will be useful when you are trying to move solder to completely seal a join.

QUENCH & CLEAN

6 Turn off the torch and use your soldering tweezers to place the tile in your quenching cup of water. After quenching, you should be able to touch it. Be sure to scrub the fire scale off with Penny Brite before soldering again on this piece. Remember, it has to be very clean and free of fire scale or the solder won't flow.

REPEAT & EXPERIMENT

7 Repeat these steps using different amounts of medium and easy solder. This will give you a feel for the different melting points and how the solders act when melted. Try to keep the hard solder from flowing when reheating your square during subsequent practice steps.

FIG. 01 FIG. 02

The trick here is to strike a balance between keeping the piece heated evenly and reflowing the hard solder. You may also want to experiment with a variety of torches if you have more than one available.

troubleshooting

✱ Remember to dim the lights before you start so you can see when the metal starts to glow.

✱ Make sure your metal is cleaned and free of fire scale between steps or else the solder won't flow.

✱ Don't heat your piece too quickly. The solder will flow best when the entire surface comes up to temperature at the same time.

✱ Solder needs to be in small pieces to flow. It's better to have several small beads than one large clump that will not melt.

SAMPLER SQUARE 7

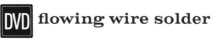 **flowing wire solder**

The idea is the same on this practice tile as on the previous one, except you are going to use wire solder. This requires the additional step of adding flux to the surface of the metal before adding the pieces of solder.

tools

Solder setup
Flush cutter
Bench block
Chasing hammer

materials

One sampler tile
Hard, medium, and
    easy wire solder
Bowl, pillbox, or
    other container
    for solder pieces
Flux and brush
Liquid dish soap

STEPS

PREPARE YOUR TILE & SOLDER

1 Remember that the surface of your tile needs to be free of dirt, grease, and fingerprints. Use soap to clean all components to be soldered, as in the last sample. When it is clean and dry, paint flux on the surface of the tile in a thin, even layer (**fig. 01**).

2 Begin by cutting your hard wire solder into little pieces, about 1–2 mm in length. These pieces should be contained in a bowl or cup to keep them from rolling all over. (See tips for organizing below). Remember to keep your hard, medium, and soft solder pieces separate.

managing wire solder

✳ Wire solder is round and likes to roll when placed on the metal. Flatten it by hammering it against a bench block with a chasing hammer before cutting.

✳ Solder needs to be cut into small pieces to melt well. Several small pieces are more effective than trying to flow one large piece.

✳ Only cut one grade of solder at a time. Gather the pieces and place them in a small container with a lid or a plastic baggie labeled with the type of solder. That way the different types won't get mixed up. Those daily pillboxes you find at the drugstore work very well for this. I just mark the letter of the solder grade on each one with a permanent marker.

APPLY THE SOLDER

3 Dip the tip of a soldering pick into the flux and then use it to pick up a piece of hard solder and lay it on the tile. This is a technique that takes a little bit of practice but is very efficient for transferring those small bits of solder. Place the solder in one corner of your tile so you have room to play with the other grades later on.

BEGIN HEATING

4 Dim the lights in your soldering area so that you can see when the metal starts to glow, as before. Turn on the torch and dry the flux slowly while bringing the tile up to temperature with slow circles at a distance of

FIG. 01

FIG. 02

6"–8" (15–20 cm) as in the last sample. If the pieces of solder jump out of place, nudge them back using the solder pick.

5 What you will observe as the metal heats:

✳ This time, there is no binder, so your piece will not flame.

✳ The flux, however, will become glassy as it heats, like an enamel coating on your tile.

✳ Fire scale should be greatly reduced because the flux is there to prevent it.

✳ As in the last sampler, you should start to see the entire piece start to glow a dull orange. This means you're ready to move to the next step.

COMPLETE THE FLOW

6 Once your piece starts to glow, bring your torch closer and focus on the solder itself, as before. You will again see it melt and become shiny. Since there is less fire scale, the solder should flow easily. The flux will also start to pool and take on a yellowish cast (**fig. 02**). This means that the solder is flowed and is a good indicator if you are unable to work in a space where you can dim the lights.

QUENCH & CLEAN

7 Just as with the last sample piece, you will need to cool your tile in the quenching cup using your solder tweezers and then remove any fire scale and the remaining flux before you try to solder again.

REPEAT & EXPERIMENT

8 Repeat these steps with medium and easy wire solder, quenching and cleaning the metal between each step. Try experimenting with different amounts of solder and different torches as in the previous square. This is your chance to play and see what works best for you!

 tip
Flux retards the amount of fire scale that forms on the surface of the metal when heated. You can also apply flux when using paste solder to prevent fire scale, but it is not necessary as flux is already in the paste mix.

troubleshooting

✳ If you are having trouble getting the solder to flow, move the torch more slowly and make sure that the sweet spot of the flame is just above the area you are soldering.

✳ As with the paste solder, try to get the medium solder to flow without melting the hard solder that is already on your tile. Then try the same thing with the soft solder. Getting a feel for this will really help you out later on with multi-step projects.

SAMPLER SQUARE 8

flowing sheet solder

Using sheet solder requires the same methods as wire solder; it's just cut differently.

tools

Solder setup
French shears or
Small scissors

materials

One sampler tile

Hard, medium, and
   easy sheet solder
Bowl, pillbox, or
   other container
   for solder pieces
Flux and brush
Liquid dish soap

FIG. 01

FIG. 02

STEPS

PREPARE YOUR TILE & SOLDER

1 Clean your tile and paint with flux as in the last sample. Use your French shears (or small sharp scissors that you will reserve for this purpose) and make a series of cuts about 1–2 mm apart and 1–2 mm deep along the edge of your solder sheet, forming a tiny fringe. Cut across the fringe to make 1–2 mm squares (**fig. 01**).

2 Store and label the squares of solder.

APPLY THE SOLDER

3 Apply a few squares of solder to your tile as before using the solder pick dipped in flux (**fig. 02**).

COMPLETE THE SAMPLER AS BEFORE

4 Begin heating, complete the flow, quench, and clean as in the last sample. You should be an old hand at this by now, so relax and have fun with it. You may find sheet solder is easier to use because it is flat and tends to stay in place.

SAMPLER SQUARE 9

one-step soldering

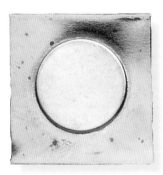

Now that you're familiar with each type and grade of solder and have a real feel for how to make them flow and behave the way you want, it's time to put them to their intended use. In this sample, you will learn the process of attaching one flat piece to another. I chose wire solder for this project, but you can also use paste or sheet solder if it makes you more comfortable. You will just need to substitute the appropriate tools for cutting and application.

tools
Solder setup
Permanent marker
Flush cutter
Bench block
Chasing hammer

materials
One sampler tile

One ½" (1.3 cm) diameter circle of 24-gauge copper or sterling silver
About six small pieces of easy-grade wire solder
Flux and brush
Liquid dish soap

STEPS
PREPARE THE TILE & APPLY THE SOLDER

1 Clean both the tile and the circle. Place the circle on the tile and trace around it with your permanent marker. Set the circle aside. Paint flux onto the tile and place the six solder pieces in the center area where the circle will go. They should be placed about ⅛" (3 mm) apart and roughly in a smaller ring within the circle you just traced. This means they should not be too close to the center or the edge (**fig. 01**). Place the circle on top of the solder chips (**fig. 02**).

FIG. 01

FIG. 02

how to deal with too much solder

If you put too much solder on your piece or if it was too close to the edge, it may flow out from under your circle and remain as a blob on the surface of your tile. This is an opportunity to learn how to remove excess solder.

✳ After quenching, cooling, and drying, you can file it away with a small file.

✳ I also like to fold a bit of wet/dry sandpaper in quarters and use the folded corner to really get into the crack against the edge of the top soldered piece. For best results, use coarse-grit sandpaper.

✳ If you have a Dremel tool, you can also use a cone-shaped carbide tip to speed up cleaning up excess solder. The tapered tip will quickly file it away. Use a light touch and a fine-grit tip.

FIG. 03

be done (**fig. 03**). Allow it to air cool for just a few seconds, then quench as before using your soldering tweezers and quench cup.

TEST THE JOIN

4 I find the best way to see if my solder join was successful or not is to pick up the completed and quenched piece and drop it on my tabletop. If the circle doesn't pop off, it worked! Congratulations on completing your first soldered join. If your circle did pop off, however, try not to get frustrated. Check out the tips below, reread any pertinent sections, clean your piece, and try again. You can do it!

BEGIN HEATING

2 Begin heating the entire piece as always, keeping your torch about 6"–8" (15–20 cm) away and moving it in slow circles.

tip
This would be a good sample to try a larger torch if you have one. The technique will work with a smaller torch, but it may take a bit longer to flow than you are used to, since you are heating two pieces of metal at the same time. Just remember to be patient and don't move the torch in too soon!

COMPLETE THE JOIN

3 When the flux is glassy and the piece starts to glow a dull red, move your torch in and begin focusing the sweet spot of the flame around the rim of the circle. Periodically sweep the flame back over the tile to keep the entire piece heated and bring it to a bright glow. You should see the circle "settle" on the tile and also see a thin molten line of solder run around the edge of the circle as the solder flows. Focus the flame for a few more seconds and you should

troubleshooting

✱ Remember that several little pieces will flow more easily than one big piece. This is especially important when using paste solder, as the temptation may be to put one big blob on at a time. I find you rarely need as much solder as you think.

✱ Be sure to take your time in the initial heating or think about using a larger torch if you have it. The challenge of this sample is getting both pieces to heat evenly together.

✱ If your join doesn't work the first time, remember to clean your pieces before trying it again.

✱ Remove extra solder with a file, a folded piece of wet/dry sandpaper, or a Dremel with a fine-grit carbide cone tip.

SAMPLER SQUARE 10
sawing & soldering a cut shape

In this sample, you will combine some techniques you have already learned with oxidation to create an eclectic patterned design. As you work through the steps in this piece, most of them should be familiar to you, but I hope you will begin to see how combining a few simple techniques can yield unexpected and eye-catching results.

tools

Permanent marker
Painter's tape
Jeweler's saw, blades, and cut lubricant
Bench pin
Jeweler's ruler or divider
French shears
Bench block
Chasing hammer
Riveting hammer, stamps, or other

texturing tool
Brass-head mallet
Liver of sulfur
A plastic spoon, disposable container, and rubber gloves
Solder setup
Pro Polish pad

materials

Two sample tiles
Easy solder of your choice (paste, wire, or sheet)

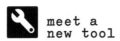

meet a new tool

Liver of sulfur

One of the ways you can bring a unique look to your jewelry components is by oxidizing them. Oxidation is a chemical change that darkens the surface of the metal, creating an antiqued look. This is a great way to highlight textures, designs, or letters on your piece; as the piece is polished, the oxidation will remain in the recessed textured areas, but be polished from the rest of the surface, creating more contrast.

There are several ways to achieve oxidation, but for this sample tile, I will focus on liver of sulfur. Liver of sulfur comes in solid (rock), gel, and liquid form. It is generally easy to use and will not rub off easily. I prefer to use the liquid or gel forms because they have a longer shelf life.

As noted in the following sampler section, you will want to mix your liver of sulfur with hot water for use. I find it best to keep this solution in a glass jar (such as a peanut butter jar). This allows you to seal it when you are done and reheat it on a coffee warmer for future uses.

SAFETY TIPS FOR LIVER OF SULFUR:

* Read and follow all manufacturer safety instructions
* Use disposable containers and utensils reserved for this purpose only.
* Use hot water from the tap or warm it on a coffee warmer as described above. Don't put it in the microwave.
* You will want to work in a well-ventilated area (Trust me on this one. It smells like rotten eggs.) You should also wear rubber gloves and safety glasses when using this chemical.
* Liver of sulfur in the bottle can be stored with your household chemicals.
* The chemical vaporizes quickly when exposed to the air, so you always want to keep it in a sealed container. To dispose of it, however, leave the solution open somewhere

starting a cut from the edge

The last time we cut with the saw we started from a hole, so the blade was already anchored in the tile. Now we are starting from the edge, so the blade may have a tendency to slip as you try to start the cut. To prevent this, you may need to anchor the blade first. Saw a little bit (a few millimeters) into the wood of your bench pin before starting on the metal. Slide the metal into position and line up the blade. Make a small introductory cut into the metal. When the cut is started you can move the metal and the saw to the center open area of the bench pin and continue your cut through just the metal.

outside (away from kids and pets). After about 24 hours, it will become clear, meaning the sulfur has evaporated. It is then safe to flush it down the toilet.

STEPS

PREPARE YOUR FIRST TILE

1 Put a piece of painter's tape across one of your tiles and draw a line of your own design with a permanent marker. This line should go all the way across but should not be in the middle of the tile. Make it about one-third of the way from one edge. I made mine wavy because it's pretty. Use your saw to cut along the line (**fig. 01**).

2 Remove the tape. You should now have two pieces with a sawed edge on each one. Trim down the larger of the two pieces by cutting ¼" (6 mm) or so off the straight edge, which is opposite the sawed edge. Use the ruler and marker (or divider) and your shears for this cut. File both pieces to finish the edges.

TEXTURE YOUR SECOND TILE

3 Set your cut tile aside and pick up the other one. Texture a section down the center using a texturing method of your choice (**fig. 02**). (See sampler square 2.)

SOLDER THE CUT PIECES TO THE TEXTURED TILE

4 Place the two cut pieces on the textured tile. If you line up the square edges with the tile underneath, there should be a gap where the texture shows through your whimsical saw cut.

5 Apply easy solder of your choice (and flux if needed) under both top pieces and solder both pieces in place at the same time. Note that you are soldering almost two whole tiles together. This amount of metal will take a

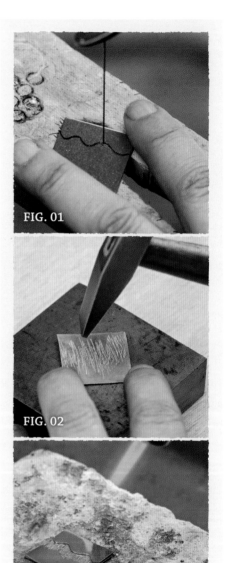

FIG. 01

FIG. 02

FIG. 03

significant amount of time to come to temperature, so be patient and use a larger torch if you have one (**fig. 03**).

6 Quench and clean the fire scale off, as always.

OXIDIZE YOUR SAMPLE

7 Take your finished sample to a well-ventilated area, put on your rubber gloves and prepare a solution of about a cup of hot tap water (not boiling) and about a teaspoon of liquid liver of sulfur. The solution should be a bright yellow color. I like to use an eyedropper to add the pure chemical to the hot water so I have more control over the amount. You can use this solution several times if you keep it in a sealed container and heat it each time. When it loses its yellow color and becomes clear, however, it will need to be replaced. (See above for storage and disposal tips.)

8 Place your piece in the solution until it darkens. If your water is quite hot, this should take about 30 seconds to a minute. The cooler the water is, the longer it will take, and liver of sulfur will work more quickly on copper than on silver.

9 Use a plastic spoon to remove your piece. Rinse in a bowl of clear water first, then under the tap. Dry thoroughly and polish the surface with a Pro Polish pad. You will note that the oxidation will be removed from the highest points first, but will remain in the cracks. You can polish it hard for a high contrast, or just go over it lightly to keep a muted tone.

oxidation tips

✱ The chemical process and scrubbing that you use to remove fire scale will also remove oxidation. For this reason, oxidation should be done last. General polishing, however, will not remove oxidation. It will only shine the piece.

✱ You can also do a quick oxidation by going over the surface of your piece with your permanent marker and then polishing it with a Pro Polish pad when dry, but this is a less permanent technique.

troubleshooting

✱ To anchor your saw for the cut, saw a little into the wood of your bench pin, then begin cutting into the metal.

✱ This tile sampler has a lot of metal. Be patient when heating and don't move in too soon. Remember to use several small, evenly spaced portions of solder, rather than one large piece.

✱ Oxidize last. Use one cup of warm tap water to about a teaspoon of liquid liver of sulfur.

✱ Dry and polish after oxidizing. The more you polish, the more contrast and shine your finished piece will have.

SAMPLER SQUARE 11

two-step soldering

This sampler is the same as the previous ones, except that you are adding an extra layer. This will illustrate the need for using progressive grades of solder in the correct order, which you have already practiced on the flow samplers. Since this piece will be three layers thick when finished, there is the added challenge of heating it evenly without reaching the flow point of the initial solder grade. By now you know what that means: slow and steady does it!

tools

Solder setup
Permanent marker

materials

One sample tile
One ¾" (2 cm) diameter circle in 24-gauge sterling or copper (I used sterling.)

One ½" (1.3 cm) diameter circle in 24-gauge sterling or copper (I used copper for this one.)
Medium solder of your choice and flux if necessary
Easy solder of your choice and flux if necessary

FIG. 01

FIG. 02

FIG. 03

STEPS

PREPARE & SOLDER THE FIRST CIRCLE

1 Start by soldering the ¾" (2 cm) circle to the tile. This is done exactly as in sampler square 9 (see page 57), except that you will be using medium solder. Here is a recap of the steps:

* Clean the tile and the circle.

* Trace the circle on the tile and then paint with flux if necessary.

* Place small pieces of medium-grade solder evenly around the inside of the traced circle not too close to the edge or the center.

* Place the circle on top and heat the entire piece slowly and evenly.

* When you see a dull glow, spend more time focusing the flame around the edge of the circle while occasionally sweeping the tile to heat the entire piece to a bright orange glow until the circle settles.

* Quench, test by dropping on your work surface, and clean to remove fire scale.

PREPARE & SOLDER THE SECOND CIRCLE

2 Place the ½" (1.3 mm) circle on top of the ¾" (2 cm) one in the center and trace around it (**fig. 01**).

3 Apply flux if necessary and place the solder as before, but this time use easy solder (**fig. 02**). Place the ½" (1.3 mm) circle on top of the ¾" (2 cm) one in the center (**fig. 03**).

4 Begin heating and complete the join as before. Be careful not to overheat the metal when you solder the second circle. You want to heat it to the flow point of the easy solder without reaching the flow point of the medium solder and loosening your original circle. As soon as you see the solder flow, remove the torch immediately. Quench, clean, and polish as always.

SAMPLER SQUARE 12

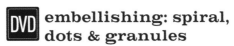

DVD embellishing: spiral, dots & granules

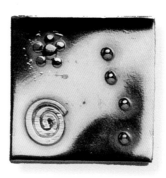

These little embellishments add a nice flair to your designs. Since these are smaller pieces, they are easily melted, so be aware of overheating! Also be careful where you are applying your solder. I used paste solder for these elements. Because they are small and may tend to roll, I find the paste solder helps them stick into place while they are heated. You will only need a tiny bit.

tools

Flush cutter
Chain-nose pliers
Bench block
Chasing hammer
Screw-down hole punch
Permanent marker
Solder setup
Brass-head mallet
Period stamp or center punch

materials

One sample tile
18-gauge copper or sterling wire
A small piece of sterling sheet in any shape, 20- or 22-gauge thick to punch dots out of
18-gauge fine silver wire
Hard, medium, and easy paste solder

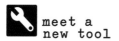

meet a new tool

screw-down hole punch

This tool has a punch at either end and punches a 2.3 mm and 1.6 mm hole. It takes a little longer than the hole-punch pliers, but it can punch through soft metal up to 16 gauge. In the next sample, we will be using the dots that it punches from the center of the hole.

STEPS

MAKE & SOLDER A WIRE SPIRAL

1 Use a flush cutter to cut a 1½" (3.8 cm) piece of 18-gauge copper or sterling silver wire.

2 Use the tip of your chain-nose pliers to grip the very end of the wire and curl the end to form a very tight loop.

3 Place the curl flat in the jaws of the pliers and grip it (**fig. 01**).

4 With your free hand, bend the wire around the pre-made curl to begin to form the spiral (**fig. 02**).

5 Release the curl and rotate it slightly, then grip it again in the pliers.

6 Continue to wrap the end of the wire around the pre-made curl, enlarging the spiral.

7 Release, rotate, and regrip in the pliers as needed. Trim excess wire using flush cutters.

8 Flatten the spiral slightly by placing it on your bench block and tapping with your chasing hammer.

9 Place a tiny bit of hard paste solder in the upper left-hand corner of the copper square. Place the spiral on top and solder as always. Quench, clean, and dry the tile.

MAKE & SOLDER DOTS

10 Use the screw-down hole punch to punch out 3–5 dots from your 20–22 gauge sterling sheet (**fig. 03**).

✳ Make a mark with your marker to position where the hole will go.

✳ Align the metal in the slot of the tool and screw the handle until the punch pierces through.

✳ Do not pull the piece of metal off of the tool, as this could break the piercing bit. Release it by turning the handle in the opposite direction until the piece of metal falls off of the bit.

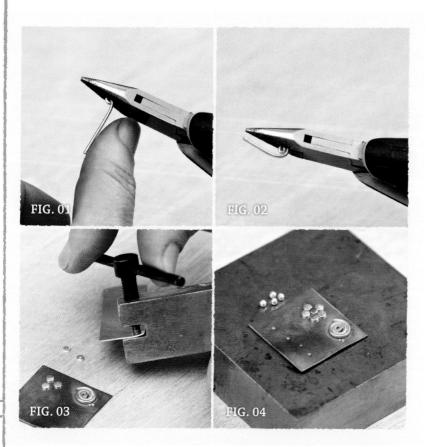

FIG. 01

FIG. 02

FIG. 03

FIG. 04

 simple soldering

64

11 If you still have the larger dot you saved from sampler square 4, you can include it with these on your tile. Place a tiny amount of medium paste solder on the back of each dot with your solder pick and place in the upper right-hand corner of the tile in whatever arrangement suits your fancy. Place, then solder, all dots at the same time. It should not take long for the solder to flow on these tiny pieces. Be vigilant and make sure you don't overheat your tile and melt the hard solder under the spiral. When the dots settle, remove the torch immediately! Quench, clean, and dry the tile again.

MAKE & SOLDER GRANULES

12 Flatten about an inch of 18-gauge fine silver wire using your bench block and chasing hammer, and cut into ¼" (6 mm) pieces. You *must* use fine silver for this step! Metal alloys will not make granules.

13 Put your tile aside and lay all four pieces of wire on your kiln brick or charcoal block with plenty of room between them. You have this block on a baking sheet with edges, right? You are about to make balls of hot metal, and balls have a tendency to roll! Make sure to take precautions so they don't roll into your lap.

14 Heat each piece separately until molten. The molten metal will naturally form itself into a round ball. Quench or allow to air cool. Use the center punch or period stamp and your brass-head mallet to make four indentations on your tile where you want to place the granules (**fig. 04**).

15 Place a 1 mm sized bit of easy paste solder on each indentation and place the granules on top. Solder all granules at once. Again, be very careful not to overheat and melt the medium or hard paste solder. The tiny amount of easy solder should flow very quickly

once you get the tile up to the point where it glows. Quench, clean, and dry as always.

solder order

Note the solder order of these pieces, from large to small. The granules are soldered last as they have the smallest contact point and are the most precarious to solder. If any of your granules do not adhere, not to worry. Simply clean the piece, apply a bit more solder, and give it another try.

troubleshooting

✳Be aware of using too much solder. If you do, and it flows out from under your embellishments, you can still file it away.

✳Always solder embellishments from large to small and from hard to easy.

✳Remember to heat the entire tile slowly from a distance. This will keep the flame from pushing small pieces (especially the granules) out of alignment.

✳Once the tile is glowing, move the torch in quickly to flow the solder and then immediately remove the heat so you don't melt your previous-grade solder.

SAMPLER SQUARE 13

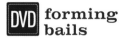 **forming bails**

Bails are attached loops used to hang pendants and earrings. In addition to its practical function, the right bail can lend to the unique and professional look of your jewelry. In this sample, we are going to learn how to make three different types of bails that you may wish to incorporate in your own designs later on. I use paste solder here as in the last sampler for the same reason: it holds these small objects in place better while heating.

tools

Tube-cutting pliers
Jeweler's ruler
Permanent marker
Jeweler's saw and
  cut lubricant
Salon board
Flush cutter
Medium Wrap n' Tap
  pliers

1.8 mm hole-punch
  pliers
Solder setup

materials

One sample tile
³⁄₃₂" (2.5 mm) rivet
  tube
16-gauge copper or
  sterling wire
Hard, medium, and
  easy paste solder

 **meet a new tool**

the third hand

This tool literally acts like another hand, ready to help you steady objects for soldering. The tweezers mounted on a swivel clamp can be moved into whatever position you need and then fixed in place by tightening the screws. They can withstand the heat of the torch without damage. The weighted base keeps the whole assembly steady while you work. As we start working on more three dimensional pieces, this tool will become indispensable.

tube bail

1 Mark a ¼" (6 mm) length on your rivet tube using your ruler and permanent marker. Use the tube-cutting pliers to cut the tube as in sampler square 4 (see page 44). File the cut ends with a fine-grit salon board. Apply a thin strip of hard paste solder along one side of the length of tube with your solder pick. Remember, you don't need much!

2 Place the tube section on the upper left-hand corner at a 45-degree angle to the edge of the copper square and solder in place (**fig. 01**).

3 Clean, quench, and dry as always.

half-loop bail

4 Use 16-gauge wire to make a 2-loop coil around the small barrel (5 mm) of the medium Wrap n' Tap pliers as in sampler 1. Use flush cutters to cut a half ring from the coil (**fig. 02**).

5 File the ends of the half loop flush with fine-grit salon board if needed. Hammer the loop flat, if necessary, using the bench block and a plastic or rawhide mallet. Place medium solder on each cut end of the half ring

FIG. 01

FIG. 02

The tweezers on the third hand are essentially a large mass of metal. They will conduct heat away from your piece while you are heating it if there is too much contact and will make it very difficult for you to get your piece up to temperature. For this reason, you want to try to grip with just the tip of the tweezers if possible. This can take some wrangling and positioning of the tool, but it is well worth it to be able to form a clean and easy solder join.

FIG. 03

FIG. 04

and place in the center of the copper square (**fig. 03**).

6 Lay the tile flat on your kiln brick and use the third hand to hold the half loop upright while soldering. You may need to elevate the base of the third hand to have it at the proper angle. You want to grip the half loop at the apex of the arch using only the very tip of the third hand's tweezers (**fig. 04**). Use a larger torch if you have one.

7 Test, quench, clean, and dry as always.

bails & pendants

I have found the half-ring and jump-ring bails to be invaluable techniques when making pendants. For thinner pieces, the jump ring can simply be punched through and soldered. For thicker pendants, the half ring can be soldered to the top edge and then a jump ring can be added through the half ring to make the pendant lie flat when worn.

FIG. 01

FIG. 02

FIG. 03

jump-ring bail

8 Use the flush cutter to cut another jump ring from the coil you made in the last step. Using your 1.8 mm hole-punch pliers, punch a hole in the bottom right-hand corner of your tile. Insert and close the jump ring (**fig. 01**). See page 39 if you don't remember how to open and close a jump ring.

9 Position the tile in a groove in the kiln brick. If your brick does not have a groove, carve out a shallow one using the point of your soldering tweezers. Set the tile in the groove so that the jump ring lies flat on the kiln brick and the join is exposed (away from the tile). Use your solder pick to place a tiny bead of easy solder on the join in the jump ring (**fig. 02**).

10 Begin heating as always; the solder should flow quite quickly, melting into the join as it does (**fig. 03**).

11 Remove your torch, quench, and clean as always.

troubleshooting

✳ On the half-ring bail, make sure the ends are completely flush for best results. Position your third hand so you only have to grip with the very tip of the tweezers and as far from the join as possible. Otherwise it will draw heat from your tile and make it difficult to bring it up to temperature. Note that you can carve a groove in your kiln brick to position your tile vertically and make it easier to solder components at different angles.

SAMPLER SQUARE 14
shaping & soldering domes

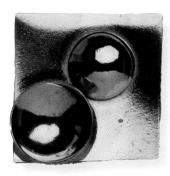

As you will see in the projects, domes add a nice bit of dimension and work well as a setting to accent beads or pearls. You will also see how to form two domes into a metal bead. In this sample, you will learn the techniques for soldering domes to a surface, both edge up (like a cup) and edge down (like a mound).

tools
Dapping block
Brass-head mallet or plastic mallet
Salon board or fine file
1.25 mm hole-punch pliers
Solder setup

materials
One sample tile
One ½" (6 mm) diameter circle blank of 24-gauge copper or sterling silver
One ¾" (2 cm) diameter circle blank of 24-gauge copper or sterling silver
Medium and Easy paste solder

 **meet a new tool**

dapping block

The dapping block curves metal circle blanks into domes and comes in both wood and metal versions. The metal block has more sizes and gives the blanks a more pronounced curve. The wooden block has depressions that are shallower. It is also more economical. If you decide to go with a wooden dapping block, be sure to read the sidebar at right.

STEPS

SHAPE THE DOMES

Shaping a flat circle into a dome is known as "dapping." You will want to do this to both your circle blanks.

1 Choose a depression in the dapping block by placing the blank in one of the depressions and checking that it can move freely (**fig. 01**).

2 Choose a punch that fits into the depression but also has a bit of room to move. Metal dapping blocks generally come with punches that match the holes exactly, so I tend to use the punch that is the next size down.

3 Lightly tap the punch using a brass head hammer to gently curve the blank. Avoid hitting the edges of the blank with the punch so they will not distort.

4 Rotate the shaft of the punch around, tapping as you go to gently coax the metal to dome in all directions. Remember that you are work-hardening it, so if it isn't cooperating, you may need to anneal your blank!

5 Continue to dome the blank gradually by moving the blank to a smaller depression and using smaller daps until the curve is to your liking.

wooden dapping block

If you are using the wooden dapping block as opposed to the metal one, you should use a plastic mallet, rather than the brass-head hammer, to hit the daps, as the heavier hammer may damage the wooden tool. If your blank becomes stuck while dapping, simply drop the entire block on your work surface from a low height and the blank should pop out again.

FIG. 01

FIG. 02

FIG. 03

FIG. 04

not vented, the heat will build up and may pop your dome off the solder (**fig. 02**).

9 Apply medium paste solder to the rim of the dome and place it back on the tile (**fig. 03**).

10 Solder as always, heating the entire piece gradually and then focusing more around the dome until the solder flows and the dome settles. Quench and clean your piece as usual.

SOLDER THE LARGER DOME EDGE UP

11 Apply a small amount of easy paste solder to the convex side of the second dome and place on the tile with the edge up so it resembles a cup (**fig. 04**).

12 Solder as before. Quench and clean as always.

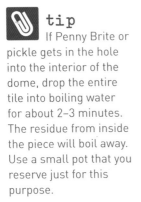

tip

If Penny Brite or pickle gets in the hole into the interior of the dome, drop the entire tile into boiling water for about 2–3 minutes. The residue from inside the piece will boil away. Use a small pot that you reserve just for this purpose.

6 Lightly file the edges of your domes, if needed.

SOLDER THE SMALLER DOME EDGE DOWN

7 Place the smaller dome on the tile with the edge down so it looks like a bump. You will want to place it off-center so you are sure to have room for the second one. Check that the fit is flush all around the edge with no gaps between the dome and the tile. If the fit is not flush, place a salon board flat on the table and file down the dome edges. Trace the dome with your marker and set it aside.

8 Drill or punch a small hole in the tile in the middle of the circle. This hole is needed to vent the heat when the dome is soldered. If it's

troubleshooting

✳ When dapping, make sure to choose a depression that allows your circle to slide around freely to start. Use a slightly smaller punch.

✳ Work the punch around the circle as you tap, being careful not to distort the edges.

✳ Move your circle to a smaller depression and continue dapping with a smaller punch to increase the curvature of your dome.

✳ If you are using a wooden dapping block, you should use a plastic mallet to strike the daps. If your dome gets stuck, simply drop the entire block on your work surface to pop it out.

✳ Remember to punch a hole when soldering a dome edge down. Remove Penny Brite or pickle from the interior by boiling in water for 2–3 minutes.

SAMPLER SQUARE 15
making a bezel & setting a stone

In this piece, I set a cabochon (a stone with a domed front and a flat back). I suggest beginning with round or oval objects that have a flat back, as they are much easier to set. Just make sure it is small enough to fit on your tile. You can also use this bezel technique on other objects besides stones. You can use a button with the shank removed, a bead that has broken in half, or any small object with this basic shape. I used wire solder for this project because it can be placed more precisely than paste.

tools
Painter's tape
Permanent marker
Millimeter gauge
Divider
French shears
Bench block
Plastic mallet
Solder setup
Burnisher

materials
One sample tile
⅛" (3 mm) plain fine silver bezel wire (not serrated)
A round or oval cabochon stone (I used an oval one that measures 10 × 14 mm.)
Hard and medium wire solder and flux
Dental floss

 meet a new tool

burnisher
The curved and pointed tip of this tool allows you to apply pressure around the edge of a bezel or setting, bending the metal around the stone to hold it in place. It works like a lever, so you shouldn't have to apply much force.

millimeter gauge
This is a sliding metal gauge that is useful for measuring when you need a quick conversion between inches and millimeters. It is also useful, as in the next sample, when a precise measurement is needed on a curved object, such as a stone or bead.

STEPS
MEASURE YOUR BEZEL WIRE FOR LENGTH & WIDTH

1 When making a bezel, the fit must be exact. To measure the length of your bezel wire, snip a piece of painter's tape so it has a square end. Wrap it around the bottom perimeter of your cabochon and mark where the end overlaps (**fig. 01**).

2 Remove the tape and place it on your bezel wire so the end of the tape lines up with the end of the wire. Cut at the mark and the wire should be the perfect length to fit around your cabochon.

3 The width of the bezel is determined by the height of the stone. Use your dividers to measure the height of the stone from the bottom edge to where the widest part of the stone begins to taper (**fig. 02**).

4 Keeping your dividers at the same width, rest one leg against the long edge of your bezel wire and draw the dividers along, scoring with the other tip. This should give you the right width of wire for your stone (**fig. 03**).

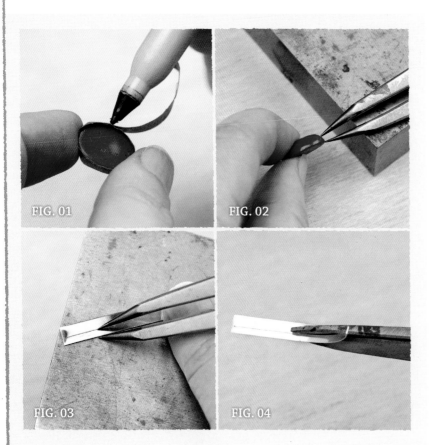

FIG. 01

FIG. 02

FIG. 03

FIG. 04

8 Paint the inside of the ring with flux and use your tweezers to stick a tiny piece of hard wire solder on the inside of the ring so that it bridges the join. It should stay in place because it is sticks to the flux (**fig. 06**).

FIG. 05

FIG. 06

FIG. 07

5 Cut the bezel wire along the score with metal shears (**fig. 04**). If your cut is not as straight as you might want it to be, you can file the bezel flush after it is soldered in a circle.

6 Hammer the wire flat, if necessary, using the bench block and plastic mallet.

CREATE THE BEZEL

7 Form the cut strip into a rough circle with your fingers and check to see that the edges are square, fitting together, and that the join is flush. File, if needed, to refine the fit, but do not take away too much metal or the bezel will be too small for the stone. A small piece of fine-grit sandpaper works well for this. Fold the sandpaper in half and press it in the join, moving it back and forth to file both sides at the same time (**fig. 05**).

simple soldering

9 Place the bezel on your kiln brick and begin heating as always. It should heat quite quickly. When the solder flows, direct your torch at the outside of the join for just a second to draw the solder through. Remember that liquid solder will always flow toward the heat (**fig. 07**).

10 Quench and clean your bezel.

FIT & PLACE THE BEZEL

11 After the bezel is soldered, push the bezel onto the stone to shape it and check the fit. The stone should slip in easily but have no visible gaps between the bezel and the stone.

SOLDER THE BEZEL IN PLACE

12 Slip the stone out of the bezel and place your soldered bezel against the tile.

13 Check the fit. If the bezel does not lie flush on the tile, place the bezel bottom-side down on a piece of fine-grit sandpaper or a salon board to file it flush. Continue checking and filing as needed until the bezel fits snugly against the tile.

14 Brush flux on the surface of the tile. Position small pieces of medium wire or sheet solder all around the inside of the bezel at about ⅛" (3 mm) intervals so they contact both the tile and the bezel. The goal is to create a continuous line of solder around the bezel (**fig. 08**).

15 Solder the piece, being careful to heat evenly all the way around the ring of the bezel. This is a good place to use a larger torch if you have one. Check the join all around to make sure that the bezel is completely soldered to the tile (**fig. 09**).

16 If there are gaps, lightly tap the top of the bezel with a rawhide hammer to close. Clean the piece before adding more flux and solder and resoldering where needed.

17 Check the top of the soldered bezel and see if it is even. If it is not, turn the tile upside down on a piece of fine-grit sandpaper and file in a circular motion until the rim of the bezel is even.

SETTING THE CABOCHON STONE

18 To test the fit of the stone, lay a piece of dental floss over the soldered bezel and push the stone into

tips for fitting the bezel

✳ If you need to make it larger, slide the bezel on a ring mandrel or bezel mandrel (see page 86) and tap it lightly all the way around using a plastic mallet.

✳ Check the fit frequently since the metal is thin and the bezel will expand quickly. If it's too large, you will need to cut it with your shears and shave it down by filing before resoldering.

FIG. 08

FIG. 09

FIG. 10

FIG. 11

tips for setting & burnishing

✳ Start by pressing the bezel against the stone in one place and then press it in on the opposite side. Continue to press the bezel against the stone on opposite sides until the bezel is tight. The bezel is less likely to become distorted using this method than if you start at one point and work your way around the stone.

✳ Be careful not to scratch the surface of the tile. Use a piece of painter's tape to protect the surface from scratches.

✳ If you don't have a burnishing tool, a curved metal teaspoon can be used in a pinch.

✳ Sometimes, if a cabochon is particularly slick and does not want to stay in place during setting, you may want to take the extra precaution of adding a bit of epoxy in the finished bezel before setting. This will secure the stone in the bezel and prevent it from slipping out.

it. The floss will keep the stone from getting stuck because you can lift up on both ends of the floss at the same time and the stone will pop out (**fig. 10**). Do not set the stone in the bezel without using this trick, as it may become stuck and almost impossible to remove without damaging the bezel!

19 If you are pleased with the fit, set the stone in the bezel without the floss and use a curved metal burnisher to press the sides of the bezel against the stone (**fig. 11**).

troubleshooting

✳ Measure the bezel wire very carefully. The fit around the stone needs to be precise.

✳ Make sure all joins are filed flush, or the solder will not fill the join. Use fine-grit sandpaper so you don't remove too much material and change the size of your bezel.

✳ Apply the solder to the inside of the bezel and then draw it through the join with your torch as it flows. Use dental floss so you can remove the stone after testing the fit.

✳ Begin burnishing by pressing on one side and then the opposite side of the bezel. Don't work your way around the bezel from a single point or the bezel may become distorted. If your bezel is lumpy or slightly distorted, you can gently smooth it by filing with fine-grit sandpaper and reburnishing the bezel to fit the stone.

SAMPLER SQUARE 16
making two small bezels & setting stones

The steps are the same for this tile as in the last one, except the bezels will be smaller in order to accommodate two stones on the tile. Smaller stones are more difficult to set because the work requires a finer touch. You will have to be very careful not to melt these bezels as you solder them together and to the tile because they are smaller. Heat slowly and use a light hand with the torch to keep them intact. This is the last sampler square because it is the most difficult, in my opinion. Don't feel bad if it takes a couple of tries to get this!

tools

Painter's tape
Permanent marker
Millimeter gauge
Divider
French shears
Bench block
Plastic mallet
Solder setup
Burnisher

materials

One sample tile
1/8" (3 mm) plain fine silver bezel wire (not serrated)
Two smaller round or oval cabochon stones (I used 6 × 7.5 mm stones for both.)
Hard and medium wire solder and flux
Dental floss

STEPS

FORM THE BEZELS

1 Follow the steps in the last sample to measure and cut your bezel wire to fit. Don't forget to file the ends. Solder them together one at a time with hard wire solder by painting the inside with flux, placing the solder piece inside with your tweezers, and then using your torch to draw it through the join as it flows. Quench, clean, and push the bezels onto the stones to reshape. File the bottoms of your bezels to fit flush with the tile.

2 Since the bezels are smaller, they can be soldered to the tile at the same time.

3 Paint the tile with flux and place both bezels. Place your medium solder on the insides against the edges as before (**fig. 01**).

4 Heat and solder both bezels in place at the same time (**fig. 02**).

5 Quench and clean.

SET THE STONES

6 Set your stones as you did in the previous sampler square. Remember to use the dental floss trick! Burnish the bezel to hold the stones in place (**fig. 03**).

7 Polish and you're done! That's it, you've just finished all the samplers!

FIG. 01

FIG. 02

FIG. 03

how to deal with a melted bezel

If the bezel melts while you are soldering it to the tile, you will need to remove it and start over. To remove the bezel, place the tip of your third hand on the tile to hold it down. Heat the entire piece until the solder flows again. Use your solder tweezers to quickly pull the bezel off. The tile can then be quenched and cleaned, the excess solder can be filed or sanded away, and you can start over with a new bezel. Of course, this may not be worth the effort to salvage a copper sample tile, but it is good practice in case this happens on an actual jewelry project.

now that you've completed your sampler

If you've gone through all the steps in this chapter, you should now have sixteen little squares, each one a testament to a new skill you've learned! If there was any technique that you found particularly daunting, you may want to revisit it. Remember, having to redo a tile is not a failure, it's just part of the learning process. That's why we practice on copper before moving to more expensive materials. After trying out your new skills on some of the finished projects in the next chapter, you should feel comfortable enough to create some wonderful designs on your own.

If you feel comfortable because these sample pieces have turned out the way you envisioned, it's time to move on to making some finished pieces. "But what can I do with my sampler?" you ask. "It seems a waste to just toss it after all that hard work!" I agree completely. You should be really proud of what you've accomplished so far. The skills you have just learned make up the heart and soul of jewelry making, and you rightly deserve to be proud of all that you have accomplished.

Here are a few ways you can use your sampler:
* Polish it and affix it to some nice matte paper and you can frame it as a conversation piece. You can also write the techniques on the back so you can use it as a reference.
* You can file down the corners and link it with jump rings by the corners for a necklace or by the sides for a bracelet or two.

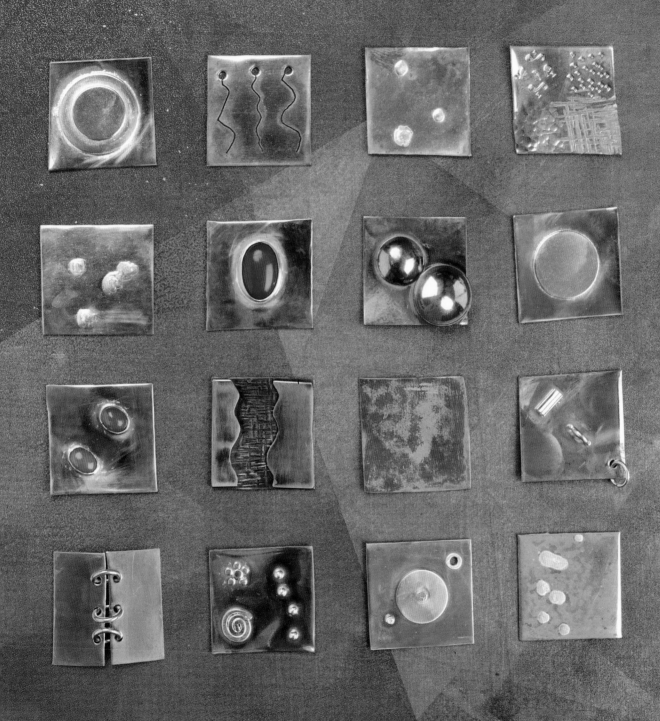

❻

the **projects**

The time has come for you to apply the skills you learned while making your sampler and create one-of-a-kind pieces of jewelry! Remember to read the whole project all the way though before starting it. And if you need to refresh your memory about individual techniques, never fear: Each project references the samplers that are its foundation. When in doubt, go back to the sampler!

The projects are presented from easiest to most challenging, and I strongly recommend that you work them in that order. But most important, get creative and have fun!

hook +eye CLASP & dapped BEAD CAPS

hook + eye clasp

TOOLS
Flush cutter (that can cut 14-gauge wire)
Medium Wrap n' Tap pliers
Chain-nose pliers
Bench block
Chasing hammer
Texture hammer, if desired
Solder setup
Liver of sulfur, if desired

MATERIALS
14-gauge copper wire, 4" (10 cm)
Easy paste solder

TECHNIQUES
Sampler square 13, Forming bails

dapped bead caps

TOOLS
Jeweler's ruler
Permanent marker
1.25 mm hole-punch pliers
Bench block
Metal dapping block
Brass-head mallet
Salon board
Pro Polish pad
Disc cutter, if desired
Texture hammers, if desired
Liver of sulfur, if desired

MATERIALS
Several circle blanks of 24-gauge copper (I used ½" [1.3 cm] ones cut from patterned sheet with a disc cutter.)

TECHNIQUES
Sampler square 2, Texturing
Sampler square 14, Shaping and soldering domes

Making your own findings is a great way to get started making projects. They're cute, quick, and add a personal touch to any larger piece. This clasp is a perfect addition to any necklace design. Simple and sleek, it can be made in a variety of sizes. The sample is a great size for necklaces that have 6mm–8mm beads. Bead caps highlight beads in a necklace design. It is important to note that dapping is the last step after texturing and punching.

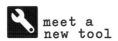

texture hammers

As we discussed in the sampler chapter, you can use a riveting or chasing hammer to texture metal, but there are also hammers specifically made for this purpose. They have a variety of patterns on the heads that mark the metal when you strike it. It is important to note that the imprint made by these hammers is a general texture and not an exact replica of the pattern on the head, as it would be with a stamp.

disc cutter

A disc cutter is a tool used to cut circles from sheet metal. It is comprised of a metal block that has holes of different diameters and corresponding cutting dies. Disc cutters vary widely in quality, and the best ones can be hard to come by. For the best results, look for a cutter that has the ability to clamp down tightly over the metal to hold it firmly in place while cutting

hook + eye clasp

1 Use the flush cutter to cut one end of the wire flush. Using the small (5 mm) barrel of the medium Wrap n' Tap pliers, make a single coil on one end of the 14-gauge wire so that the ends overlap (**fig. 01**). Cut a jump ring with your flush cutters, being sure to flip the cutters to make both ends of the ring flush. Set aside.

2 Cut the end of the remaining wire flush and make a loop at one end using the small (5 mm) barrel of the Wrap n' Tap pliers (**fig. 02**).

3 Measure ⅜" (1 cm) from the top of the loop you just made. Grip the wire at that point with the large barrel of the Wrap n' Tap pliers and curve the wire up and over the pliers to create a hook (**fig. 03**).

4 Cut the excess wire away with the flush cutter so that the end of the hook is even with the bottom of the loop.

5 Grasp the tip of the wire at the end of the hook with your chain-nose pliers and give it a slight forward bend to help flare the hook (**fig. 04**).

6 Place both the hook and the eye on your bench block. Hammer lightly with the chasing hammer to flatten slightly. The hook can gain a nice dimensional quality if you flatten only the loop, high arc of the hook, and flared tip. If desired, texture the metal with a texturing hammer or one of the tools discussed earlier.

7 To make the loop sit flush against the wire for soldering, open it slightly as you would a jump ring. Use the flush cutter to cut the wire

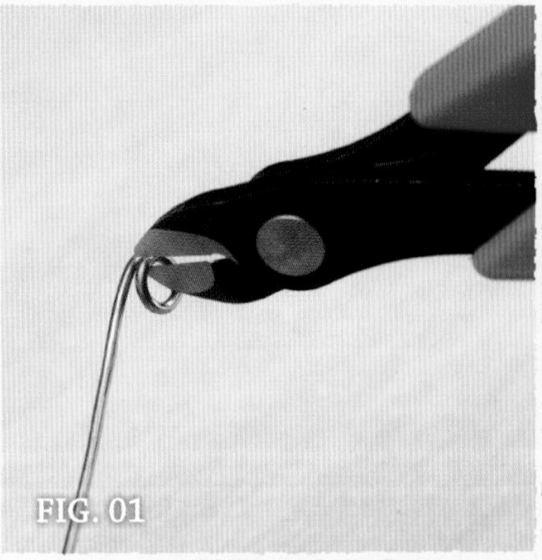

FIG. 01

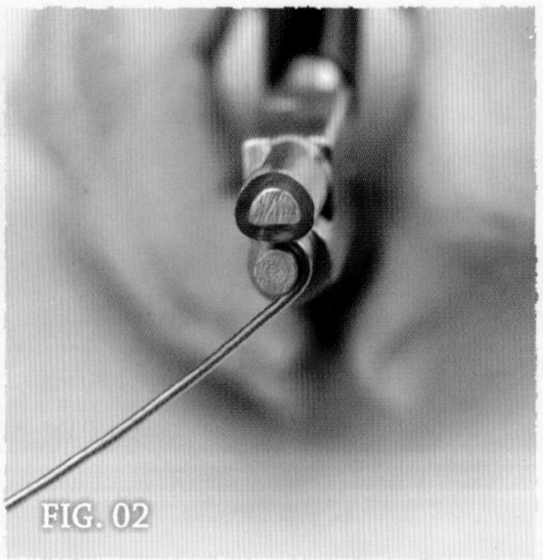

FIG. 02

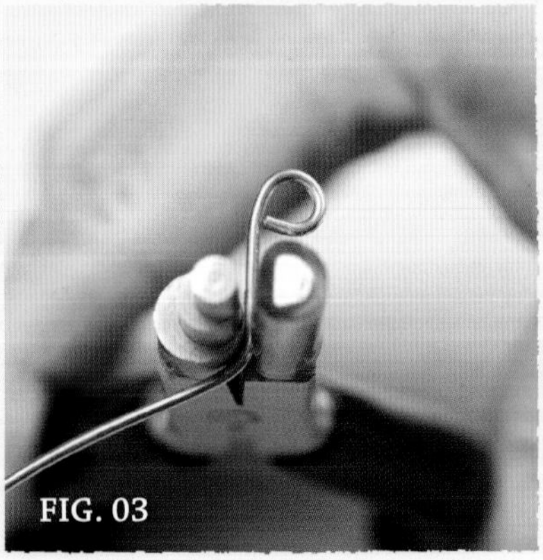

FIG. 03

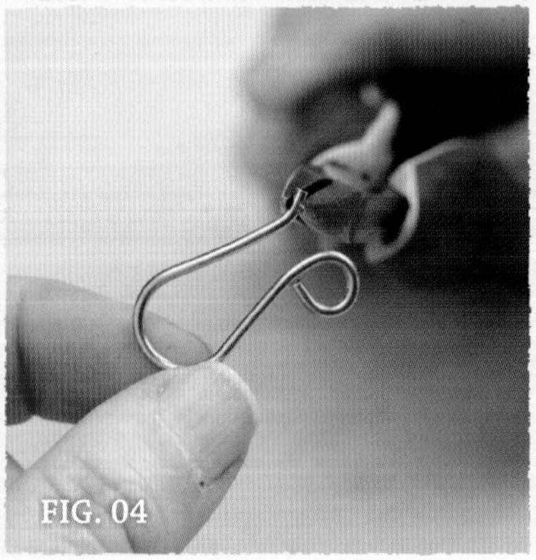

FIG. 04

at a slight diagonal—so it will sit snugly against the side of the hook (**fig. 05**). Close the loop.

8 Place both pieces on your kiln brick. Apply solder to the join in the ring and the join in the loop at the bottom of the hook (**fig. 06**).

9 Turn on your torch and begin heating. When the binder has burned away and the pieces start to glow, move in close and focus the flame more over the solder (**fig. 07**).

10 The solder should melt into the join. Remove your torch and quench both pieces.

11 Clean the pieces. If desired, oxidize with liver of sulfur and polish with a Pro Polish pad.

📎 **tip**
For a design variation, you could replace the eye portion of the clasp with a second hook.

DVD **dapped bead caps**

1 Begin with precut discs or cut your own using a disc cutter. I base mine on the size of the bead. There is no hard and fast rule regarding bead cap to bead size ratio. You want to be sure that the caps are noticeable but don't overwhelm the bead.

2 If you are using plain discs or sheet, you may want to texture them with stamps or texture hammers. The ones in this project are made from prepatterned copper sheet.

3 After the discs are textured, find the center of the circle using the chart on page 155. Mark and punch a hole using the 1.25 mm hole-punch pliers (**fig. 01**).

4 Lay your circle pattern-side down in the dapping block and dap.

5 Repeat for remaining discs.

6 Oxidize with liver of sulfur, if desired, and polish with a Pro Polish pad.

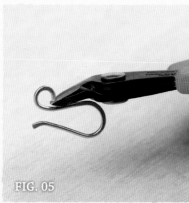
FIG. 05

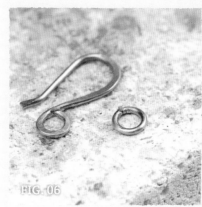
FIG. 06

FIG. 07

FIG. 01

📎 **tip**
When you dap, you want to keep the edges of the dome as neat as possible. Take care not to dap too close to the edge, or it will splay. This may be a cool effect if you want it, but when you are making bead caps, you need to keep the edges even.

stacked
RINGS

TOOLS

Ring mandrel
Large Wrap n' Tap pliers
Flush cutter
Salon board
Solder setup
Pro Polish pad
Chasing hammer
Chain-nose pliers
Bent-nose pliers

MATERIALS

12" to 18" (30.5 to
   45.5 cm) of 14-gauge
   sterling silver wire
Small scrap of 18-gauge
   fine silver wire (about
   ½" [1.3 cm])
Easy and hard paste
   solder

TECHNIQUES

Sampler square 1,
   Connecting metal using
   jump rings
Sampler square 12,
   Embellishing: Spiral,
   dots, and granules
Sampler square 13,
   Forming bails

These simple rings will give you a basis for working on the more complex designs later on. By the time you finish, you should be comfortable working on the ring mandrel and have an idea how to solder and size rings. It requires a bit of precision to place the solder and granules on the ring (which is standing straight up as you solder it), but you can do it! These rings will look great with just about any outfit.

large wrap n' tap pliers

These pliers are the same design and function as the medium Wrap n' Taps used earlier in sampler square 1 (see page 37). The only difference is that they have larger barrels that are most often used for rings (13 mm, 16 mm, and 20 mm).

ring mandrel

This is a steel cone marked with the standard ring sizes. It is useful as a sizing tool and as a kind of round bench block for hammering, texturing, or stamping on finished rings.

STEPS

1 To figure out your ring size, take a ring that fits you well and slide it onto the ring mandrel. Remember the mark where it stops. This is your ring size and will be used in all future ring projects (**fig. 01**).

2 Grip the very tip of your 14-gauge wire in the jaws of the Wrap n' Tap so it is against the middle (16 mm) part of the coiling jaw. Hold tightly with the pliers and rotate the handles away from you about a quarter turn to begin to form a loop (**fig. 02**).

3 Open the jaws and rotate the pliers back toward you, renewing the grip farther back along the wire. Twist the tool away from you again to continue the coil. Use your free hand to guide the wire as it feeds into the tool.

4 Repeat this process. With each twist and release the wire continues to bend around the jaw. Be sure that the end of the wire you are holding in your free hand goes behind the emerging coil (closer to the pliers' handles) to give it room to grow. Make a coil of about six loops into a 16 mm coil. (**NOTE:** *If you have very small fingers, you might want to start on the smallest barrel.*)

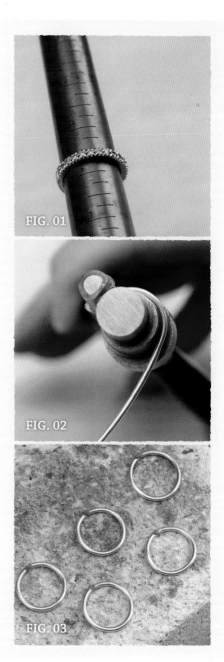

FIG. 01

FIG. 02

FIG. 03

5 Take the coil off the pliers and slide it onto the ring mandrel. As you push it down it will uncoil and expand in diameter. Do this until it is about half a size smaller than your desired size. (It will expand a little more as you continue to work it.)

6 Using your flush cutter, cut five rings off your coil. Be sure to flip the cutter over with each clip to ensure a flush cut at the ends you will be joining. File if necessary.

7 Using your chain-nose and bent-nose pliers, gently twist and wiggle the ends of the ring back and forth, pushing lightly until they are past each other. Twist them again and gently pull back: they should pop into place. Look at the join from several angles to be sure the ends of the ring match up exactly and are not offset. Do this with all the rings.

8 Apply hard paste solder to the join of all the rings and place them on your kiln brick so the joins are all facing away from you (**fig. 03**).

9 Turn on your torch and begin heating. When the binder has burned away and the pieces start to glow, move in close and focus the flame more over the solder. The solder should melt and flow into the join. Just do one ring right after another (**fig. 04**). The solder should flow quickly. Quench, clean, and dry all the rings.

10 Take each of your finished ring bands and place them on the ring mandrel. Tap them gently all the way around, slightly flattening them and increasing them to your desired size. (**NOTE:** When you do this with rings that have wider bands in later projects, you will want to flip them around on the mandrel frequently, so they don't take on its tapered shape.) When all five rings bands are the desired size, set aside.

11 Cut three ⅛" (3 mm) pieces from your 18-gauge fine silver wire. Place them on your kiln brick. Turn on your torch and heat slowly until they melt and form granules.

12 If you haven't already done so for previous projects, scrape out a small slot in your kiln brick with the tip of your soldering tweezers. Place one of your ring bands in this divot seam-side down. Apply a tiny bit of easy paste solder to the top of the ring band and top with one of the granules (**fig. 05**).

13 Solder as above, quench, clean, and repeat with two more of the rings.

14 Use your salon board to file the soldered seams smooth. Polish using a Pro Polish pad or in a tumbler.

FIG. 04

FIG. 05

Large Wrap n' Tap pliers
Flush cutter
Ring mandrel
Solder setup
Round-nose pliers
Chain-nose pliers
Bench block
Chasing hammer
Pro Polish pad

MATERIALS

16-gauge wire, sterling
    silver, 1 ft. (30.5 cm)
20-gauge wire, sterling
    silver, 6" (15 cm)
Semiprecious briolette
    beads, 2
26-gauge wire, sterling
    silver, 6" (15 cm)
Easy paste solder

TECHNIQUES

Sampler square 1,
    Connecting metal using
    jump rings
Sampler square 4, Riveting
Sampler square 13,
    Forming bails

simple chain
EARRINGS

This project not only makes great earrings but also could be elongated into a necklace with multi-sized links. You might also try altering the look of the earrings by wire wrapping briolette drops on each link for a fuller look. There are no limits here—let your imagination run wild!

STEPS

1 Coil the 16-gauge wire three times around the middle step (16 mm) of the large Wrap n' Tap pliers. Remove the coil from the pliers and slide it on to your ring mandrel. As you push it down the mandrel the coil will expand with the cone. Slide it down to the size 8 line (18 mm). Remove and cut coil into two links. Use the flush cutter to cut the ends of the links flush as with a jump ring.

2 Continue to use the large Wrap n' Tap pliers to make two more rings on the center barrel (16 mm) and two rings on the small barrel (13 mm).

3 Lay the set of large (18 mm) rings and the set of small (13 mm) rings on the kiln brick near each other. Apply easy paste solder to each join and solder all four rings closed. (You can do them one at a time, but I find it's easier to do them all at once.) Quench and clean.

4 Connect the large and small soldered rings together with a medium (16 mm) ring. Set up this ring for soldering by placing the two previously soldered rings in a groove in the kiln brick so the two soldered rings are perpendicular to the brick and the ring to be soldered lies flat. Add easy paste solder to the join on the medium ring (**fig. 01**).

5 Solder closed. Note that you can use any grade of solder here because these are actually separate pieces. Just concentrate the flame on the center ring only. The result is a set of three connected rings in graduated sizes.

6 Repeat for second set of rings. Clean both sets of rings.

7 To flatten the rings, place one ring at a time on the edge of a bench block and strike with the flat end of a chasing hammer rotating the ring as you go to flatten the entire ring. You want to do this after soldering because doing it before soldering might ruin your flush surfaces.

8 Wire wrap a semiprecious briolette on the small link on each earring with the 26-gauge wire:

✱ Thread the wire through the opening in the briolette, leaving a short end of ⅝" (1.5 cm) and long end of 1¾" (4.5 cm). Cross the ends over each other (**fig. 02**).

✱ Using your chain-nose pliers, gently pinch the X where the wires cross (**fig. 03**) and gently align the wires side by side (**fig. 04**).

✱ Gripping the base of the longer wire with your pliers, bend the wire to a 90-degree angle (**fig. 05**).

✱ Switch to your round-nose pliers. Grip the wire in the 90-degree angle and bring the wire up and over the top barrel (**fig. 06**).

✱ Switch to your round-nose pliers. Grip the wire in the 90 degree angle and bring the wire up and over the top barrel. Complete the loop (**fig. 07**).

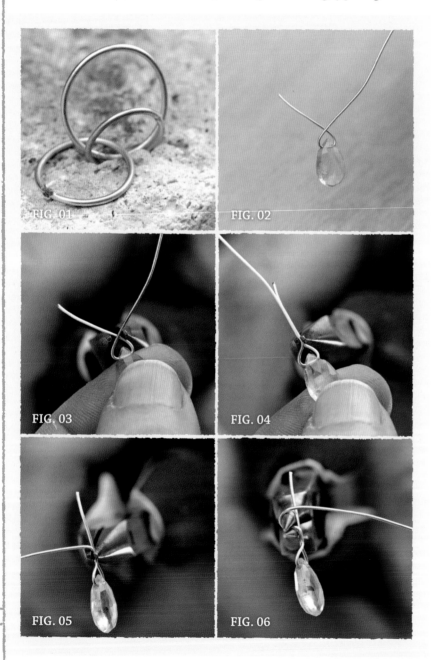

FIG. 01
FIG. 02
FIG. 03
FIG. 04
FIG. 05
FIG. 06

✱ Slide the loop onto the smallest soldered ring and wrap closed (**fig. 08**).

✱ Grip with your chain-nose pliers and continue wrapping (**fig. 09**). Trim ends.

9 To make ear wires, cut your 20-gauge wire in half to make two pieces that are 3" (7.5 cm) each. Use your torch to draw a bead on the end of each wire as you did when making the balled rivet in sampler 4.

10 Use the round-nose pliers to curve the ball end of the ear wire back onto itself to form a U-shape. Measure ¾" (2 cm) from the top of the ball. Grasp the wire at that point with the largest barrel of the medium Wrap n' Tap pliers and curve the wire up and over the head to form a hook. Bend the tip of the wire out at a slight angle with your chain-nose pliers to flare the hook. Repeat with second wire. (See Hook + Eye Clasp, page 80.)

11 Place the ear wire on the bench block and tap along the curve to flatten slightly.

12 Attach the large loop of the earring chain to the ear wire by opening the

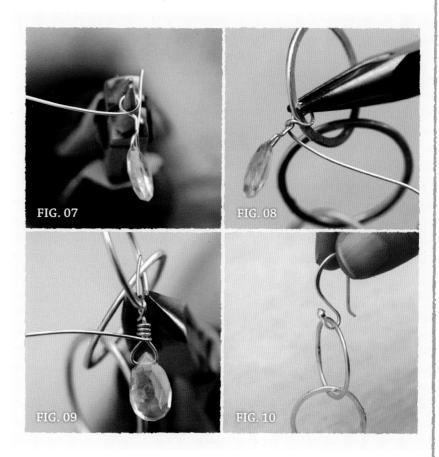

FIG. 07

FIG. 08

FIG. 09

FIG. 10

U-shape slightly by twisting to the side as you would a jump ring. Slide chain into the U-shape (**fig. 10**) and pinch closed with chain-nose pliers.

13 Polish using a Pro Polish pad. Repeat for second earring.

soldered
BEADS

Soldered beads are fantastic elements to incorporate into almost any design. This bead is also used in the Pearl Chain Earrings project (see page 94). I often use beads as focal pieces strung with other beads in necklaces or bracelets. You can make one at a time or go into production mode and make several at once. It's fun to have several beads of all different textures to choose from as you're working.

This bead is also used in the Pearl Chain Earrings project (see page 94).

TOOLS
1.25 mm hole-punch pliers
Solder setup
Riveting hammer, texture hammer, center punch, or stamps, etc. (for texturing).
Dapping block (A metal one works better for this project, but wood is okay, too.)
Brass-head mallet
Salon board
Disc cutter (If you're cutting your own discs)

MATERIALS
4 discs of 24-gauge copper and/or sterling, ¾" (2 cm) (You can buy these pre-made and textured or cut your own out of plain or patterned sheet, as I did, using a disc cutter.)
Easy paste solder

TECHNIQUES
Sampler square 2, Texturing
Sampler square 14, Shaping and soldering domes

1 Cut and texture the discs as desired. For the silver bead, I textured the metal first with the long end of the riveting hammer in a radiating pattern. Then I used the period stamp to make a cross pattern of dots in a straight line down and across the center of the bead, then continued in a random pattern over the entire surface. The copper bead is cut from pre-patterned copper sheet. If you don't have pre-patterned sheet, texture the disc to your liking. Remember to avoid texturing the edges so that they will stay smooth for soldering. If they become distorted, use the salon board to gently file them back to a flush edge.

2 Find the center of the circle on one of the blanks using the guidelines on page 155. Mark and punch the center of the circle with the 1.25 mm hole-punch pliers. Lay this disc on top of its corresponding mate and mark through the hole with a fine-tip permanent marker for the second hole and punch. Repeat for the second set of discs.

3 Select one set of discs and dap them into domes of equal curvature. (Use the same depression on the block for both.) Remember to be careful not to distort the edges. Repeat with the second set of discs.

4 After dapping, place the set of domes against each other and check the seam. If needed, place each dome edge down on a salon board that is flat on a table surface. Move the piece back and forth across the salon board to true up the edge.

5 Choose one set of domes. If you haven't already, carve out a shallow indentation in the surface of your kiln brick so it holds the bead steady for soldering.

6 Place one dome edge up in the depression and apply easy paste solder around the rim (**fig. 01**).

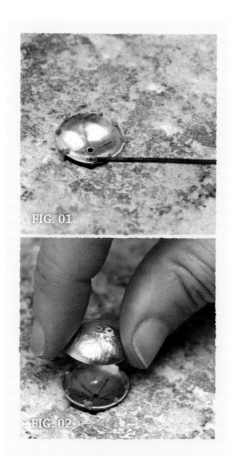

FIG. 01

FIG. 02

7 Carefully add the second dome on top, lining up the edges (**fig. 02**).

8 Turn on your torch and begin heating. When the binder has burned away and the pieces start to glow, move in close and focus the flame more over the solder. The solder should melt and flow into the join. Remove your torch and quench both pieces, then clean. Remember you can remove pickle from the interior by immersing the pieces in boiling water for 1–2 minutes.

9 Repeat with the second set of domes.

check the seam

Hold the bead up to the light and check to see that the seam is completely soldered all the way around. If there is a gap, place the bead in a depression in the metal dapping block and give it a couple of light taps with the plastic mallet to close the gap. Add just a tiny amount of solder along the join and re-solder. File away any extra solder along the seam with a salon board.

TOOLS

1.25 mm hole-punch
  pliers
Solder setup
Chasing hammer
Bench block
Metal dapping block
Brass-head mallet
Salon board
Disc cutter, if cutting
  own discs
Round-nose pliers
Chain-nose pliers
Flush wire cutters
Medium Wrap n' Tap
  pliers

MATERIALS

Two brass soldered
  beads (made on
  page 92)
Four freshwater pearls,
  6mm
18-gauge sterling silver
  wire, 8" (20.5 cm)
20-gauge sterling silver
  wire, 6" (15 cm)
Easy paste solder

TECHNIQUES

Sampler square 1,
  Connecting metal
  using jump rings
Sampler square 4,
  Riveting
Sampler square 13,
  Forming bails

pearl chain
EARRINGS

This project combines simple soldered beads, wire-wrapped pearls, and soldered links to create a great earring with a lot of movement and swing. This same technique without the soldered bead could also be adapted as a linked bracelet or necklace chain. I find it easier to make all the components separately before assembling the earrings.

STEPS

1 Make the soldered beads: Follow the directions in the previous project for making a pair of soldered beads.

2 Make the head pins: Cut two pieces of 18-gauge wire at 1½" (3.8 cm). Draw a bead on the end of the wire by holding it in your tweezers at a slight angle and directing your torch flame at the lower quarter from the side. When the wire starts to glow, move the angle of the torch to focus the sweet spot of the flame directly at the end of the wire. When the ball forms, flick the flame up the wire and then remove it. Quench and clean. For more detailed instructions, see sampler square 4 (see page 44). Make a ball on the other wire and set both aside. These wires with balled ends are now head pins.

3 Assemble the beads and head pins: Place one soldered bead on one of the 18-gauge balled head pins. Bend the wire at a right angle

with your chain-nose pliers. Measure ⅜" (1 cm) from the angle and cut away the excess wire. Use the round-nose pliers to bend the wire up and around until it meets the place where you bent it at a right angle, forming a loop (**fig. 01**).

4 Flatten the loop by placing it on the edge of the bench block and tapping it gently with a hammer. Repeat with the second bead and set both aside.

5 Make the jump-ring links: With the remaining length of 18-gauge wire, use the small (5 mm) barrel of the Wrap n' Tap pliers to make a six-loop coil. Use the flush cutters to make six jump rings from the coil. Close all the rings and lay them out on the kiln brick. Solder the rings closed with easy paste solder, quench and clean, then set aside.

6 Make the ear wires: Cut the 20-gauge wire in half so you have two pieces at 3" (7.5 cm) each. Draw a bead on each of these as above.

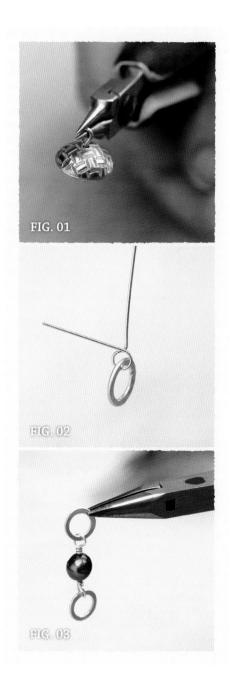

FIG. 01

FIG. 02

FIG. 03

Use the round-nose pliers to curve the ball end of the ear wire back onto itself to form a U-shape. Measure ¾" (2 cm) from the top of the ball. Grasp the wire at that point with the largest

THE SAME TECHNIQUE WITH-OUT THE SOLDERED BEAD COULD ALSO BE ADAPTED AS A LINKED BRACELET OR NECKLACE CHAIN.

barrel of the medium Wrap n' Tap pliers and curve the wire up and over the head to form a hook. Bend the tip of the wire out at a slight angle with your chain-nose pliers to flare the hook. Repeat with the second wire. (Follow the directions in the previous project for making ear wires.)

7 Make the wire-wrapped components: Choose a soldered ring. Make a wire wrapped loop (see page 157) and, before finishing the wrap, slide the ring through the loop (**fig. 02**).

8 Slip a freshwater pearl onto the wire. Bend the wire, making a second wire-wrapped loop. Thread a second soldered ring onto the wire before closing the loop (**fig. 03**).

9 Repeat until you have a short chain consisting of three soldered rings and two wire-wrapped pearl units.

10 Repeat with the second set of components. Attach the ear wires to one end of each earring. Open the loops on the head pins you made earlier, like a jump ring, and attach your soldered beads to the other end of the earrings.

11 Oxidize with liver of sulfur if desired and use a Pro Polish pad to polish (liver of sulfur will not damage the pearls).

TOOLS

Rivet hammer
Bench block
Solder setup
Power-punch pliers
Metal dapping block
Brass-head mallet
Medium Wrap n' Tap
  pliers
Flush cutter
Salon board
Liver of sulfur
Pro Polish pad
Round-nose pliers
Chain-nose pliers

MATERIALS

1" (2.25 cm) circle of 24-
  gauge sterling silver
Small tag with a top loop
  (I used a ½" (1.3 cm)
  scalloped circle tag.)
5/16" (8 mm) circle of 24-
  gauge sterling silver
  (I punched one out of
  a scrap of sheet using
  power-punch pliers.)
1/8" (3 mm) of 18-gauge
  fine silver wire
1" (2.5 cm) of 18-gauge
  sterling silver bead
  wire with 1mm beads
1" (2.5 cm) of 24-gauge
  sterling silver wire (or
  pre-made head pin)
One freshwater pearl,
  6mm
Hard, medium, and easy
  paste solder

TECHNIQUES

Sampler square 1,
  Connecting metal
  using jump rings
Sampler square 2,
  Texturing
Sampler square 11,
  Two-step soldering
Sampler square 12,
  Embellishing: Spiral,
  dots, and granules
Sampler square 13,
  Forming bails
Sampler square 14,
  Shaping and soldering
  domes

pearl
dangle
PENDANT

This is a classic vintage-style piece that combines a number of elements to create the finished look. Its delicateness is by no means plain; the numerous components, especially the textured metal, gives it depth and interest. You can use any tag you want as long as it's flat. If you don't have a tag, you can use hole-punch pliers to make a hole directly in the pendant for your jump ring.

STEPS

1 Place the 1" (2.5 cm) sterling circle blank on your bench block and tap with the tapered end of the riveting hammer to texture.

2 Place the textured circle on your kiln brick. Apply small dots of hard paste solder to the tag and place on top of the circle so that the loop on the tag hangs off the circle (**fig. 01**).

3 Turn on your torch and begin heating. When the binder has burned away and the pieces start to glow, move in close and focus the flame more over the tag. The solder should flow and the tag should settle. Remove your torch and quench. Set this piece aside.

4 Use the power-punch pliers to punch a ⁵⁄₁₆" (8 mm) circle out of a scrap of 24-gauge sterling sheet (or use a pre-made circle blank).

5 Place this small circle in your metal dapping block and dome it slightly. (You will need a metal block for this, as the wooden ones do not have small enough depressions.) Set aside.

6 Place your ⅛" (3 mm) piece of fine silver wire on your kiln brick and heat with the torch until it melts and forms a granule.

7 Place the textured circle with the tag on it in your dapping block, texture side up, and dome slightly. Tap lightly when you are dapping so you do not mar the metal or break the solder join. If the loop at the top of the tag bends while dapping, gently straighten it using your chain-nose pliers.

8 Place the pendant on your kiln brick, textured side up. Place a small amount of medium paste solder on the small dapped circle and then place the granule inside.

9 Put medium paste solder on the tag and place the cup and granule on the tag portion of the pendant, edge up (**fig. 02**).

10 Heat and solder the entire piece as above. The granule should now be soldered to the cup and the cup to the pendant.

11 Use the small (5 mm) barrel of the medium Wrap n' Tap pliers to make a coil out of the bead wire. Cut a jump ring using your flush cutter. As always, remember to flip the cutter between cuts so that both ends of the ring are flat.

12 Rotate the ring open and put it through the exposed loop on the pendant. Rotate it closed. Place the pendant upright in a slot in your kiln brick so that the jump ring lies flat on the kiln brick. The seam in the jump ring should be as far from the pendant as possible. Place a small amount of easy paste solder on the join in the jump ring (**fig. 03**).

13 Solder, quench, and clean. File away any excess solder with a salon board.

14 Oxidize using liver of sulfur, if desired, and polish.

15 If you don't have a pre-made head pin, make one out of the 24-gauge sterling wire. Draw a bead by holding the wire in your tweezers at a slight angle and direct your torch flame at the lower quarter from the side. When the wire starts to glow, move the angle of the torch to focus the sweet spot of the flame directly at the end of the wire. When the ball forms, flick the flame up the wire and then remove it. Quench and clean.

16 Place the pearl on the head pin and then wire wrap it to the jump ring. (For wire wrapping instructions, see page 157.)

FIG. 01

FIG. 02

FIG. 03

TOOLS

Jeweler's ruler
Permanent marker
Large Wrap n' Tap
   pliers
Flush cutter
Ring mandrel
Bench block
Chasing hammer
Metal dapping block
Brass-head mallet
Salon board
Sandpaper
Solder setup
Third hand
Table vise
Riveting hammer

MATERIALS

14-gauge sterling silver
   wire, 18" (45.5 cm)
24-gauge sheet or three
   ⁵⁄₁₆" (8 mm) diameter
   circles

Three 24-gauge × 1"
   (2.5 cm) sterling
   silver head pins
16-gauge fine silver
   wire, ¼" (6 mm)
Two freshwater pearls,
   4mm
Liver of sulfur
Easy, medium, and
   hard paste solder

TECHNIQUES

Sampler square 1,
   Connecting metal
   using jump rings
Sampler square 12,
   Embellishing: Spiral,
   dots, and granules
Sampler square 13,
   Forming bails
Sampler square
   14, Shaping and
   soldering domes

pearl+ silver
5-STACK RINGS

These elegant and simple rings incorporate elements of soldering and riveted beads. I love wearing mine to jewelry shows, where they always get a lot of comments. In this case, more is definitely more! Using the table vise in conjunction with the ring mandrel is a great way to keep rings steady for texturing, stamping, or riveting.

meet a new tool

table vise

A table vise is the perfect tool for holding objects still while you work. I recommend getting one with a clamp, so you can secure it to your worktable and move it as needed. Many of them also have swiveling heads that are helpful for securing your work at different angles.

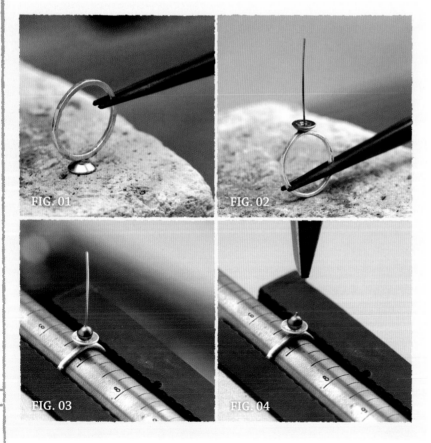

FIG. 01

FIG. 02

FIG. 03

FIG. 04

STEPS

1 Use the 14-gauge wire to make a six-loop coil on the small barrel (13 mm) of the large Wrap n' Tap pliers.

2 Size the rings: You will want this coil to end up two sizes smaller than the finished rings because they will become further enlarged during flattening later on. To size the coil, slide it down the ring mandrel to the mark two sizes smaller than the desired end result. The coil will unwind some as the inner diameter increases.

3 Once the coil is the desired size pull the coil off the mandrel and cut five rings from the coil using a cutter, flipping the cutter to keep the ends of the rings flush. File ends flush if needed.

4 Put two of the rings on your kiln brick. Apply hard paste solder to the joins. Turn on your torch and begin heating. When the binder has burned away and the pieces start to glow, move in close and focus the flame more over the solder. The solder should melt and flow into the join. Remove your torch and quench the rings. Repeat with the other three rings. Clean and dry all five rings.

5 Place each ring on the ring mandrel and tap all the way around the band using a chasing hammer. The ring will flatten and increase in diameter. Flip the ring on the mandrel each time it grows a half size. Tap the ring until it has grown two full sizes or until the desired size is reached. Place each ring on the bench block. Use a chasing hammer to tap each ring on both sides until the wire of the band is square.

6 Cut three ⁵⁄₁₆" (8 mm) or ¼" (6 mm) circles from the 24-gauge sheet using a disc cutter. You can also use pre-made blanks or circles punched with your power-punch pliers.

7 Use the dapping block to dap each circle into a dome. You will need a metal dapping block for this step because the wooden blocks do not come with small enough depressions. Remember to use your brass mallet with the disc cutter and metal dapping block!

8 Place one dome edge down on the kiln brick. Add medium paste solder to the back of the dome. Use the third hand to position one of the ring bands over the top of the dome and hold it in place so that the original solder join on the band is facing up (opposite the join between the band and the dome). Remember to grip the ring with the very tip of the third hand's tweezers as far from the new join as possible (**fig. 01**).

9 Follow the steps above to solder. Quench, clean, and repeat with two of the other rings. You should now have three rings with cups and two without. Polish and set the two plain rings aside.

10 Place your piece of 16-gauge fine silver wire on your kiln brick and heat it to form a large granule as in sampler square 12 (see page 63).

11 Grip one ring in the third hand, dome up. Place easy paste solder in the bottom of the dome with the granule on top. Solder as above, heating slowly and being careful not to remelt the granule. Quench, clean, and polish this ring.

12 Place a second ring in the third hand, dome up. Place easy solder in the bottom of the dome and heat with the torch. Hold one head pin in the soldering tweezers and as the solder melts place head of the head pin in the center of the dome, flat end down. Quickly remove the torch. The

FOR A DIFFERENT LOOK, TRY MIXING THE METALS IN THIS PIECE OR USE A DIFFERENT SEMI-PRECIOUS ROUND BEAD.

head pin should now be soldered in cup of the dome (**fig. 02**). Quench, clean, and polish this ring, using a light touch so as not to bend or break the wire. Repeat these steps with a third ring.

13 Place one of the rings with the head pins on the ring mandrel and clamp the mandrel tightly in your table vise with the head pin sticking up. Place a pearl on the head pin (**fig. 03**).

14 Cut away excess wire leaving a scant 1/16" (2 mm) wire above the hole. Use a riveting hammer to gently splay the wire, rivet the pearl in place (**fig. 04**). Repeat with the other head-pin ring.

15 Oxidize all the rings with liver of sulfur if desired. Polish with a Pro Polish pad.

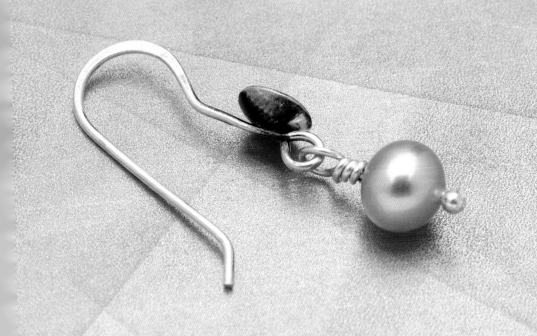

TOOLS

Power-punch pliers
Flush cutter
Metal dapping block
Brass-head mallet
Solder setup
Chasing hammer
Bench block
Liver of sulfur
Round-nose pliers
Medium Wrap n' Tap
pliers
Chain-nose pliers

MATERIALS

Two 24-gauge sterling
silver circles, 9/32"
(7 mm) (or punch
your own out of scrap
sheet with the power-
punch pliers)
Two pieces of 18-gauge
fine silver wire, 1/8"
(3 mm) each
6" (15 cm) of 20-gauge
sterling silver wire
Medium and easy paste
solder
Two pieces of 1" (2.5 cm)
× 24-gauge sterling
silver wire (or pre-
made head pins)
Two freshwater pearls,
6mm

TECHNIQUES

Sampler square 4,
Riveting
Sampler square 12,
Embellishing: Spiral,
dots, and granules
Sampler square
14, Shaping and
soldering domes

pearl dangle
EARRINGS

This is a little fancier variation on a basic ear wire. Since the ear wire itself is embellished, I chose to keep the earring simple by adding a single wire-wrapped pearl. The result is both sophisticated and fun. In making it, you are building on the techniques from previous projects and taking them one step further.

STEPS

1 Use the power-punch pliers to make two circles that are $\%_{32}$" (7 mm) out of 24-gauge sterling sheet or use pre-made blanks. Place these circles in your metal dapping block and dome. Set aside.

2 Place your two pieces of 18-gauge fine silver wire on your kiln brick. Heat with your torch until they melt and form granules.

3 Place both cups you made in step one on your kiln brick edge up. Apply a small amount of medium paste solder in each cup. Place the granules, one in each cup. Turn on

your torch and begin heating. When the binder has burned away and the pieces start to glow, move in close and focus the flame more over the solder. The solder should flow, allowing the granules to settle. Remove your torch, quench, and clean both pieces. Be careful not to overheat and remelt the granules.

4 To make ear wires, cut your 20-gauge wire in half to make two pieces that are each 3" (7.5 cm) long. Measure about $\%$" (1.5 cm) from one end of each of these wires and tap here with the ball of the chasing hammer to flatten slightly. This will be the surface on which you will solder the granule cups.

5 Use your solder tweezers to make two very shallow divots in the surface of your kiln brick. Lay the wires in these divots. Apply a small amount of easy paste solder to the outside of each granule cup and place them so they sit on the flattened portion of each wire (**fig. 01**).

6 Solder as above, quench, and clean. Oxidize with liver of sulfur if desired.

7 Use the round-nose pliers to curve the end of the ear wire nearest the granule cup back onto itself to form a loop. The end of the wire should be touching itself just behind the cup (**fig. 02**).

8 Measure 1" (2.5 cm) from the other end of the wire. Grasp here with the largest barrel of the medium Wrap n' Tap pliers and curve the wire up and over the head to form a hook (**fig. 03**).

9 Cut away any extra wire; the wire should be even with the loop. Bend the tip of the wire out at a slight angle with your chain-nose pliers to flare the hook.

10 Repeat with the second wire. Tap the curves of both hooks gently with your chasing hammer on the bench block to flatten slightly.

11 If you don't have pre-made head pins, you can make your own by holding one of the 24-gauge sterling wires in your tweezers at a slight angle and directing your torch flame at the lower quarter from the side. When the wire starts to glow, move the angle of the torch to focus the sweet spot of the flame directly at the end of the wire. When the ball forms, flick the flame up the wire and then remove it. Quench and clean. For more detailed instructions, see sampler square 4 (see page 44). Repeat with the other wire.

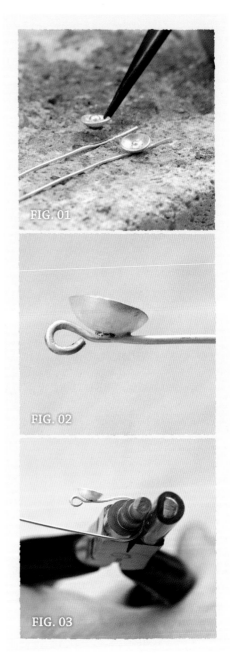

FIG. 01

FIG. 02

FIG. 03

12 Slide the pearls onto the head pins and wire wrap to the loops at the bottom of the ear wires. (See page 157 for instructions on wire wrapping.)

soldered
key PENDANT

This is a great three-dimensional pendant that has a lot of room for creative interpretation. Think about using other metals for the flat ends of the key, personalizing with your initials, or creating your own patterns for the shape of the "bit" and the "bow."

STEPS

1 Trace or photocopy the patterns for the bow (loop at the top of the key) and the bit (part that goes in the lock) in the back of this book (see page 155). Paste them onto a sheet of 20-gauge copper with rubber cement and saw them out. Remember to use lubricant and anchor your blade in the bench pin before beginning your cut. Peel the paper off these pieces and file all the edges and corners. Stamp a dot on either side of the bow and one more at the tip of the bit. These will be settings for granules to be soldered on later (**fig. 01**).

2 Use the larger punch of the screw-down hole punch to make a hole at the top of the bow. Set both of these pieces aside.

3 Use your ruler and permanent marker to mark your rivet tube at 1⅛" (2.8 cm). Grip in your tube-cutting pliers and cut the tube to the correct length.

4 Grip the tube in your tube-cutting pliers again and brace one end against your work surface. Using your jeweler's saw, cut a slit through the middle of one end of the tube. The slit should be ⅛" (3mm) deep (**fig. 02**).

5 Check to see if the tab on the piece you cut out for the bow of the key fits in this slot. Enlarge the slot with the saw as necessary (**fig. 03**).

6 Turn the tube around in the pliers and re-grip. You may wish to mark the direction of the slot with a permanent marker first to be sure that it is parallel to the slot you cut in the last step. Cut another slit in this end for the bit of the key. Check for fit and enlarge with the saw if necessary. Be careful of making these slots too big. The end pieces should just slide in.

7 Slide both end pieces into the slots you made in the tube and place on your kiln brick. Make sure all the dots you stamped are on the same side. Use your solder pick to push small amounts of hard paste solder inside the ends of the tube and against the tabs on the bow and bit. If any solder smears to the outside of the tube, be sure to wipe it away before heating.

8 Turn on your torch and begin heating. If you have a Max Flame torch, this is a great time to use it. When the binder has burned away and the pieces start to glow, move in closer and focus the flame more over

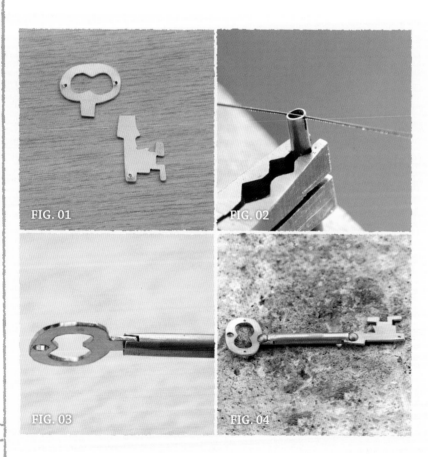

FIG. 01

FIG. 02

FIG. 03

FIG. 04

the end pieces of the key. The solder should melt and flow into the join. Remove your torch, quench, and clean. File away any excess solder if necessary.

9 Use your ⁵⁄₃₂" punch on the power-punch pliers to cut two circles out of your 24-gauge copper. Place these circles in your metal dapping block and dome.

10 Apply small amounts of medium paste solder to the edges of these domes. Place them edge down on the ends of the key so they are just touching the tube (**fig. 04**).

11 Solder, quench, and clean as above. Since they are very small, there is no need to punch holes to vent the heat as you normally would with larger domes.

12 Place the three pieces of fine silver wire on your kiln brick and heat with your torch until they melt and form granules.

13 Apply small amounts of easy paste solder to each of the granules and place them in the dots on the bow and bit of the key. Solder as above, quench, and clean.

14 Using the smallest (5mm) barrel of the medium Wrap n' Tap pliers, make a loop out of the bead wire. Cut the ends flush with your flush cutter. Rotate this ring open and put it through the hole you punched in the bow of the key. Place the key upright in a groove in your kiln brick so that the ring lies flat on the brick. The seam of the jump ring should be as far from the key as possible. Apply a small amount of easy paste solder to the join. Solder, quench, clean, dry, and file, if necessary.

15 Oxidize in liver of sulfur and polish with a Pro Polish pad.

YOU CAN SCALE DOWN THIS
PATTERN TO MAKE A SMALLER
KEY. MAKE SEVERAL IN
DIFFERENT SIZES AND HANG
TOGETHER AS A PENDANT.

TOOLS

Permanent marker
Jeweler's ruler
Jeweler's saw and
    cut lubricant
Bench pin
Power-punch pliers
Tube-cutting pliers
Bench block
Chasing hammer
Needle files
Flush cutter
Metal dapping block
Brass-head hammer
Solder setup
Center punch
Riveting hammer
Medium Wrap n' Tap
    pliers
Salon board
Liver of sulfur
Pro Polish pad
Chain-nose pliers (for
    long pendant)

MATERIALS

*For small flower
pendant*

1" × ¾" (2.5 × 2 cm)
    blank of 20-gauge
    sterling silver (or
    cut from a sheet)
³⁄₃₂" (2.5 mm) rivet
    tube (I used copper.)
2" (5 cm) of 12-gauge
    copper wire
Scrap of 24-gauge
    sheet (to punch
    ³⁄₁₆" (5 mm) discs
    out of)
Two pieces of
    18-gauge fine
    silver wire, ⅛"
    (3 mm) each
2" (5 cm) of 14-gauge
    copper wire
Rubber cement and
    paper (for sawing
    template)

Hard, medium, and
    easy paste solder
*For long flower
pendant*
¾" × 1⅝" (2 × 4 cm)
    blank of 20-gauge
    sterling silver (or
    cut from a sheet)
⅛" (3 mm) rivet tube
4" (10 cm) of
    16-gauge copper
    wire (for branches)
Nine pieces of
    18-gauge fine
    silver wire, ⅛"
    (3 mm) each
2" (5 cm) of 18-gauge
    copper wire (for
    jump ring)
Rubber cement and
    paper (for sawing
    template)
Hard, medium, and
    easy paste solder

TECHNIQUES

Sampler square 1,
    Connecting metal
    using jump rings
Sampler square 2,
    Texturing
Sampler square 4,
    Riveting
Sampler square 9,
    One-step soldering
Sampler square 10,
    Sawing and
    soldering a cut
    shape
Sampler square 12,
    Embellishing:
    Spiral, dots, and
    granules
Sampler square 13,
    Forming bails
Sampler square 14,
    Shaping and
    soldering domes

tube-riveted
PENDANTS

This pendant involves a lot of
small pieces. Be sure to have a bowl
handy to keep them together!
Both of these pendants are made
essentially the same way with
slight variations. I have included
complete instructions for making
the smaller one, along with the
measurements and materials
required for the longer pendant.

STEPS

SMALL FLOWER PENDANT

1 Start with a pre-made rectangle blank of 20-gauge silver or cut your own from 20-gauge sterling sheet. To do this, use your ruler and permanent marker to measure and draw a 1" × ¾" (2.5 × 2 cm) rectangle on the paper. Use rubber cement to adhere the paper to the surface of the metal sheet. Place the sheet on your bench pin and saw out the shape with your jeweler's saw. (This metal is too thick for shears.) Remember to apply lubricant to your saw blade and support the saw in the bench pin before beginning to cut the metal. Peel the paper off the finished piece, then file down the edges and corners. I also slightly rounded the edges on mine to give it a softer look.

FIG. 01

FIG. 02

FIG. 03

2 Use your power-punch pliers to punch a 3/32" (2 mm) hole in one end of the rectangle, about 1/8" (3 mm) away from the edge. Put the rivet tube through the hole so about 1/32" (.5 mm) is above the surface of the sheet. Make a mark on the tube about 1/32" (.5 mm) from the other side of the sheet. (The total length of the tube up to the mark should be about 1/8" [3 mm].) Place the tube in the jaws of the tube-cutting pliers so the mark lines up with the slot in the jaws. Use your saw to cut the tube. Set the tube and the rectangle aside.

3 Place your 12-gauge piece of copper wire on your bench block and tap it flat with a chasing hammer. File down and round the edges and corners of both ends of the flattened wire with your needle files. (See **fig. 01** for the difference between rounded and not rounded.) Use your flush cutter to cut off about 1/8" (3 mm) at a slight angle. Set this little piece aside.

4 Use your file to round the end of the wire where you just cut. Cut another piece that is about 3/16" (5 mm) long and set aside. Round the end again and cut off a piece that is about 1/2" (1.3 cm) long. This last cut should be straight across, rather than angled. Round the bottom of the 1/2" (1.3 cm) piece where you just cut. This piece will become the main stalk of the flower. Set aside and discard the excess wire.

5 Use your Power Punch pliers to punch two 3/16" (5 mm) discs out of 24-gauge sterling. Place these in your metal dapping block and dome slightly. Set aside.

6 Place your two pieces of fine silver wire on your kiln brick and heat with your torch until they melt and form granules.

7 Lay your sterling rectangle on your kiln brick. Apply small bits of hard paste solder to the small pieces of flattened copper wire

FIG. 04   FIG. 05

you made previously. Arrange them on the rectangle in the form of branches, with the angled ends of the shorter wires against the main "stalk."

8 Turn on your torch and begin heating. When the binder has burned away and the pieces start to glow, move in closer and focus the flame more over the flattened wires. The solder should flow and the "branches" should settle. Remove your torch, quench, and clean the pendant (**fig. 02**).

9 Place the pendant back on the kiln brick. Place a small amount of medium paste solder in each of the domes you made previously and place your granules in the domes. Place medium paste solder on the back of each of the domes, then place them, edge up, at the ends of two of the branches (**fig. 03**).

10 Solder as above, being careful to heat evenly and not melt the granules. The granules should now be soldered to the cups, which should be soldered to the pendant. Quench and clean the piece once again.

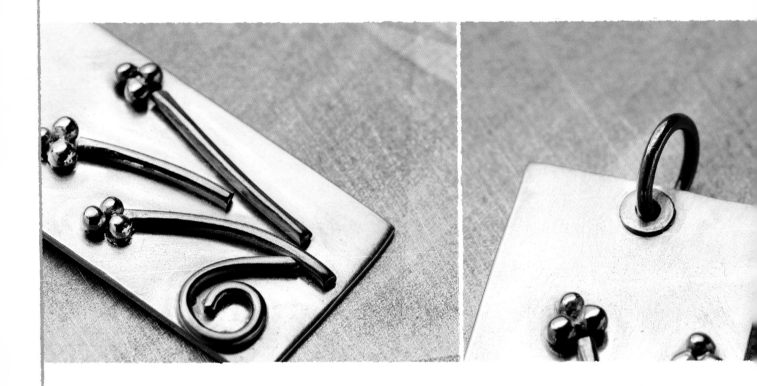

THESE TAG PENDANTS ARE A
PERFECT STARTING POINT FOR
YOUR OWN DESIGNS.... LET YOUR
IMAGINATION RUN WILD—STAMP
AND EMBELLISH AWAY!

11 Use your center punch to stamp three dots at the end of the remaining branch. I used my permanent marker for placement before stamping (**fig. 04** on page 115).

12 Put the rivet tube through the hole in the pendant. Place the pendant and the tube on your bench block. Insert the center punch in the end of the tube and gently tap with the brass-head hammer to flare the rivet. Repeat on the other side. Finish flattening the rivet with the flat face of the rivet hammer (**fig. 05** on page 115).

13 Use the 14-gauge copper wire to make a loop around the middle (7mm) barrel of the medium Wrap n' Tap pliers. Cut a ring with your flush cutter, being sure to flip the cutter so both ends of the ring are flush. File the ends if necessary.

FIG. 06

14 Rotate the ring open, place it through the tube rivet, and rotate closed again. Make sure the ends of the ring line up in all directions.

15 Place the pendant on its edge in a slot in your kiln brick so the ring lies flat on the surface of the brick with the join as far from the pendant as possible. Apply a small amount of easy paste solder to the join in the ring and solder as above. File off any excess solder with a salon board, quench, and pickle.

16 Oxidize with liver of sulfur, if desired, and polish with a Pro Polish pad or tumbler.

LONG FLOWER PENDANT

17 Cut and file the rectangle as above. Punch the hole for the tube rivet (it will be ⅛" [3 mm] for this one). Measure and cut the tube for the rivet as above.

18 Make nine granules from the fine silver wire as above and set aside.

19 Cut four pieces to be "branches" from the 16-gauge copper wire. (I cut three pieces at ¾" (2 cm) each and one ½" (1.3 cm) piece.) Don't flatten the wires as above but use your fingers and chain-nose pliers to bend them and form one of the longer pieces into a spiral. Just make sure there is room for all of them on your pendant. I find it easier to draw the design on the pendant with permanent marker and then bend and cut the pieces to fit (**fig. 06**).

20 Solder the pieces to your pendant. I soldered all the copper branches in one step with hard solder, then all the granules with medium solder. Remember to make indentations for the granules with your center punch to help keep them in place while soldering.

21 Make the tube rivet and jump ring as above. Use easy solder to solder the jump ring. File, clean, oxidize, and polish as above.

TOOLS

Permanent marker

Screw-down hole
punch

Period stamp or center
punch for texturing

Bench block

Brass-head mallet

Solder setup / Max
Flame torch

Metal dapping block

Jeweler's saw and cut
lubricant, or shears

Bench pin

Slash stamp

Round-nose pliers

Chain-nose pliers

Large Wrap n' Tap
pliers

Ring mandrel

PowerMax flush cutter

Salon board

Chasing hammer

Liver of sulfur

Pro Polish pad

MATERIALS

Small 24-gauge flower
blank. (I used one
that measured
about ½" (1.3 cm)
with 5 petals.)

Scrap of 24-gauge
sterling sheet (for
punching dots and
sawing leaf)

10-gauge gold-filled
wire, about 3"
(7.5 cm)

Rubber cement and
paper

Hard, medium, and
easy paste solder

TECHNIQUES

Sampler square 1,
Connecting metal
using jump rings

Sampler square 2,
Texturing

Sampler square 10,
Sawing and
soldering a cut
shape

Sampler square 11,
Two-step soldering

Sampler square 12,
Embellishing:
Spiral, dots, and
granules

twining vine
RING

This is an adjustable ring that incorporates gold-filled wire. Care needs to be taken when heating gold-filled because you don't want to melt through the outer gold layer. The soldering portion of this project also includes small pieces placed on the ends of the band. This means you need to be careful to heat the piece slowly. Coming in close with your torch too soon could blow these pieces right off. If this happens, just clean and try again.

meet a new tool

powermax flush cutter

These are the big guns of the wire cutter world. They are useful for cutting heavy-gauge and flat wire that would damage other cutters, making them essential tools for ring bands and other projects involving thick wire.

STEPS

1 Use the screw-down hole punch to make 3 dots from your scrap of 24-gauge sterling silver sheet.

2 Use the period stamp or center punch to stamp a dot on each petal of the small flower blank.

3 Place the flower blank on your kiln brick and apply a tiny amount of hard paste solder to the back of each of the dots you cut in step one. Place the dots in the center of the flower blank. Turn on your torch and begin heating. When the binder has burned away and the pieces start to glow, move in close and focus the flame more over the solder. The solder should flow and the dots settle. Remove the torch, quench, and clean.

4 Place the flower blank with dots in your metal dapping block and dome slightly. Set aside (**fig. 01** shows a flat flower and a domed flower).

5 Trace or photocopy the leaf template from page 155. Use rubber cement to apply the template to your 24-gauge sterling sheet. Cut out the shape using your jeweler's saw or shears. Remember to stabilize the saw in the bench pin before beginning your cut.

6 Use the slash stamp to make the veins on the leaf. I did a center vein, three smaller veins on one side, and two on the other. I suggest drawing the pattern with your permanent marker before stamping.

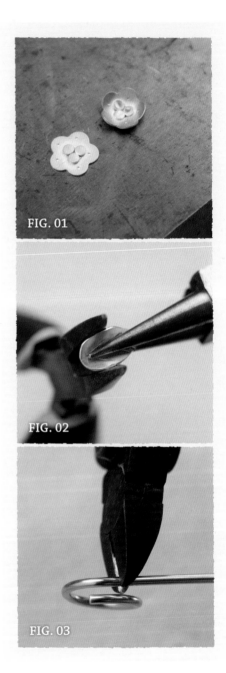

FIG. 01

FIG. 02

FIG. 03

7 Grip the leaf along the line of the main vein with your round-nose pliers. Grip the edges with the chain-nose pliers as shown (see photo) and gently push it into a bowed leaf shape. Set aside (**fig. 02**).

8 To save wire (gold-filled is expensive!) I worked with the coil and didn't cut the ring band until the end to make sure there was no scrap. Start by making a loop on the middle (16 mm) barrel of the large Wrap n' Tap pliers. Make sure the loop overlaps by at least ½" (1.3 cm). Take the loop off the pliers without cutting it and place it on your ring mandrel. Slide it down the mandrel to expand it to your desired ring size. Mark the wire with your permanent marker, leaving about ¼" (6 mm) of overlap. Remove from the ring mandrel and cut with the PowerMax Flush cutter (**fig. 03**). Make sure the flat side of the cutter is positioned toward the inside of the ring to give it a flush end. File if necessary.

FIG. 04

FIG. 05

FIG. 06

9 Put the band back on the ring mandrel and tap it sparingly with the ball end of the chasing hammer. You want to add a little texture to the band without enlarging the ring. Hammer a little more on the ends to flatten slightly for soldering (**fig. 04**).

10 Rotate the ring open slightly. Place it on your kiln brick in a slot (carve one with your soldering tweezers if needed) so that it sits upright with both ends up.

11 Apply medium paste solder to one end of the band and place the dapped flower on top (**fig. 05**).

12 Solder as above, using the Max Flame torch, if you have one. This one takes some patience, so be sure to heat the entire piece very slowly before moving in to flow the solder, otherwise the flower might fall off. If the flower begins to move, coax it back into place with a solder pick (**fig. 06**). Quench, clean, and place back on the kiln brick in the same position.

13 Solder the leaf on the other end of the band with easy paste solder. Again, be patient and heat slowly! Quench, clean, and oxidize before polishing with a Pro Polish pad. (The liver of sulfur will only affect the silver portions. The gold filled ring band will remain shiny.)

copper tube BEAD

This bead is perfect for showcasing prepatterned metal sheet. You can also texture your own using hammers and metal stamps. I like the effect that the mixed metal gives the design. This single bead is perfect as a centerpiece. After you have made a couple, try scaling them down and make several into a necklace or bracelet.

STEPS

1 Use the dividers to mark the smooth side of the copper sheet 2" (5 cm) in from the edge and cut with your French shears. Use the dividers and shears again to cut this strip to ¾" (2 cm) wide so that you have a piece that measures ¾" × 2" (2 × 5 cm). Hammer flat on your bench block with a plastic mallet, if necessary, taking care that you don't damage the pattern.

2 Anneal the metal. Patterned metal can be very stiff and will work-harden quickly, so you will need to anneal before, and possibly during, shaping.

the piece starts to glow, move in close and focus the flame more over the solder. The solder should melt and flow into the join. Remove your torch, quench, and pickle, then dry.

6 Slide the tube onto a ring mandrel and tap lightly with a plastic mallet. Flip the bead over and repeat. Since the mandrel is tapered you don't want to hammer the tube into a cone shape. Frequent tapping and flipping will help to avoid this. Set aside. This tube is the center section of the bead.

7 Use precut blanks and texture or use the disc cutter to cut two ⅝" (1.5 cm) diameter circles and two ¾" (2 cm) diameter circles from patterned brass strip. File any rough edges with fine-grit sandpaper.

8 Find the center of the circles using the template in the back of this book (see page 155). Use the 1.25 mm hole-punch pliers to punch holes in the center of each blank.

9 Place one ¾" (2 cm) diameter circle pattern-side down in the coordinating depression in the dapping block and dap into a dome. Repeat for second circle.

10 Apply hard solder paste to the edge of one domed circle and place it on top of a flat ⅝" (1.5 cm) circle on your kiln brick. Check to see that the holes are lined up and that the two pieces are centered (**fig. 02**).

11 Solder as before, quench, and clean. Repeat with the remaining circle set. Remember to immerse in boiling water for a minute or two to remove cleaning residue and debris from the interior. (Do not reuse this pot for food.)

12 There are now three components that need to be soldered together to make the bead. Place the copper tube upright on the kiln brick. Apply medium solder to the rim of the tube and center one end cap unit on top. Check the placement to see that it is centered. Solder and pickle as before.

3 Use a pair of chain-nose pliers and a pair of bent chain-nose pliers to bring the two short ¾" (2 cm) ends of the metal together, shaping the metal strip into a tube. If needed, you can also tap the metal around a ring mandrel using a plastic mallet and then use the pliers to help close the tube and refine the shape (**fig. 01**).

4 Use your fingers to close the ends of the tube. Flush together by pushing one end of the tube up and over the other and then pull back into place. The edges should pop together under tension and form a flush seam. File with fine-grit sandpaper folded over to refine the seam if needed. If your shape is a bit wonky at this point, don't worry. It can be refined after soldering.

5 If you haven't cleaned after annealing, do so now. Apply hard paste solder to the inside of the tube with your solder pick. Place the tube on your kiln brick on one end with the seam toward you. Turn on your torch and begin heating. When the binder has burned away and

simple soldering

FIG. 01

FIG. 02

FIG. 03

USE PLAIN SHEET FOR A SLEEKER LOOK OR STAMP YOUR OWN DESIGNS.... FOR ANOTHER DESIGN VARIATION, TRY SOLDERING THE ROUND DOMED PIECE TO THE OPENINGS IN THE TUBE WITHOUT THE FLAT WASHER.

13 This side is a little trickier to solder, but I know you can do it. Use your chain-nose pliers to carve a shallow depression in the surface of the kiln brick. Place the component that you just soldered dome-side down so it sits in the depression in the brick and is stabilized (**fig. 03**).

14 Apply easy paste solder to the upturned rim of the bead, center the second end cap on top, and solder. Clean the bead one last time, and boil to remove any excess compound from the interior.

15 Oxidize the bead if desired with liver of sulfur and polish.

TOOLS

Permanent marker
Ruler
Jeweler's saw and cut
    lubricant
Bench pin
Divider
French shears
Bench block
Chasing hammer
Chain-nose pliers
Round-nose pliers
Millimeter gauge
Flush cutter
Liver of sulfur
Pro Polish pad
Solder setup

MATERIALS

20-gauge sheet silver
    at least ¼" × 1" (.6 ×
    2.5 cm)
Rubber cement and paper (if
    sawing your own blank)
One round stone, 4.5 mm
⅛" (3 mm) wide plain fine
    silver bezel wire
Painter's tape
Hard, medium, and easy
    wire solder / flux
Easy paste solder
Dental floss
2" (5 cm) of 18-gauge
    sterling silver bead wire
    with 1mm beads

TECHNIQUES

Sampler square 1,
    Connecting metal using
    jump rings
Sampler square 10,
    Sawing and soldering
    a cut shape
Sampler square 13,
    Forming bails,
Sampler square 16,
    making two small bezels
    and setting stones

ruby tag
PENDANT

This is a simple but classic pendant that incorporates a set stone. Be sure to use dental floss when testing the stone in the bezel and don't do the final setting and burnishing until all the soldering is finished! The heat from the torch could thermal shock and damage your stone.

steps

1 Use a pre-made blank or cut the tag out of 20-gauge sheet with your jeweler's saw. To do this, use your ruler and permanent marker to measure and draw a ¼" × 1" (.6 × 2.5 cm) rectangle on paper, then use rubber cement to adhere the paper to the surface of the metal sheet. Place the sheet on your bench pin and saw out the shape with your jeweler's saw. (This metal is too thick for shears.) Remember to apply lubricant to your saw blade and support the saw in the bench pin before beginning to cut the metal. Peel the paper off the finished piece and file down the edges and corners.

2 Use the painter's tape to measure around your stone. Use your divider and French shears to trim the width of the wire, if necessary. Form the bezel and file the ends flush if necessary.

3 Place the bezel on your kiln brick. Paint the inside with flux and place a tiny piece of wire solder inside the join with your tweezers. Turn on your torch and begin heating. When the flux has become glassy and the pieces start to glow, move in closer and focus the flame more over the solder. The solder should melt and flow into the join. Move your torch to the outside of the bezel to draw the solder through quickly and then remove the flame. Quench and clean.

4 Fit the bezel around the stone for size and to give the bezel its final shape. Remove the stone after sizing.

5 Place the ¼" × 1" (.6 × 2.5 cm) blank on your kiln brick and paint with flux. Place the bezel about ⅛" (3 mm) from one end (**fig. 01**).

6 Apply small grains of medium wire solder around the inside of the join. Solder as above, quench, and clean.

7 Test the fit of the stone in the finished bezel using the dental floss trick. Don't set the stone yet! Remove it after sizing and set aside.

8 Use your millimeter gauge and permanent marker to make a mark on the jaw of your round-nose pliers where they are ³⁄₁₆" (5 mm) thick. Make a loop with your bead wire around this point and cut half a ring as in Sample 13 (see page 66). Make sure the ends of this half loop are flush.

9 Lay the pendant flat on your kiln brick. Apply a tiny amount of easy paste solder to both ends of the half ring of bead wire and lay it against the pendant to create a bail on the end opposite the bezel (**fig. 02**). Solder as above, quench, and clean (**fig. 03**).

10 Use the same mark on your round-nose pliers to make a full jump ring out of the bead wire. Cut the ends flush and put it through the bail you just created. Set the pendant on its side in a slot in your kiln brick and make sure the join in the jump ring is as far from the bail as possible (**fig. 04**). Apply a small amount of easy paste solder to the join in the ring and heat, being careful not to melt the solder that holds the bail on. Quench and clean as always.

11 Place your pendant on your work surface and set the stone by burnishing. Remember to start in one place and then work back and forth across the bezel rather than around to prevent distortion.

12 Oxidize using liver of sulfur, if desired, and polish with a Pro Polish pad.

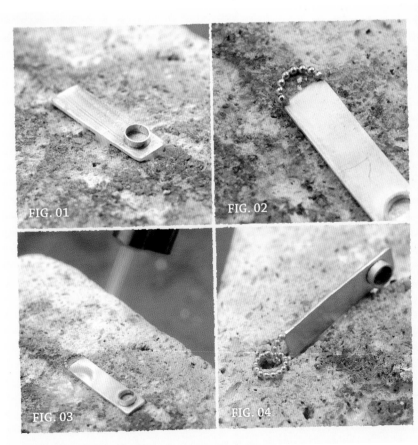

FIG. 01

FIG. 02

FIG. 03

FIG. 04

TOOLS

Large Wrap n' Tap pliers
PowerMax or heavy-duty
    flush cutters
Ring mandrel
Solder setup / Max Flame
    torch
Chasing hammer
Fine-grit sandpaper
Salon board
Bench block
Jeweler's ruler
Chain-nose pliers
Brass brush
Pro Polish pad
Liver of sulfur (optional)
Tumbler and shot
    (optional)

MATERIALS

10-gauge sterling silver
    wire, 6–7" (15–18 cm)
18-gauge fine silver wire,
    at least 1¾" long
    (4.5 cm)
Hard, medium, and easy
    sheet or wire solder/flux
Liquid dish soap for
    polishing

TECHNIQUES

Sampler square 5, Work-
    hardening, annealing,
    and cleaning fire scale
Sampler square 12,
    Embellishing: Spiral,
    dots, and granules
Sampler square 13,
    Forming bails

midcentury modern RING

With clean lines and just a hint of embellishment, this ring is eye-catching yet understated. Fabricate each ring, one step after the other, to ensure that the rings will be the same size. Anneal the ring while sizing to make it easier to stretch the ring to size. Some steps of this ring are tricky, but don't panic! You'll see in the instructions how to fix the most common pitfalls.

steps

1 Anneal the 10-gauge wire as in sampler 5.

2 For sizes 6, 7, 8: Use the small barrel (13 mm) of the large Wrap n' Tap pliers to make a two-loop coil with the annealed wire. For sizes 9, 10, 11: Use the middle barrel (16 mm) of the Wrap n' Tap pliers.

3 Pull the coil off the Wrap n' Tap and cut it into two rings using the PowerMax cutter. Be sure to flip the cutter with each clip to keep the ends of the rings flush. File if necessary. Clean.

4 Place both rings on the kiln brick and apply flux and hard solder to the inside of the seams. Turn on your Max Flame torch and begin heating. When the flux has become glassy and the pieces start to glow, move in closer and focus the flame more over the solder. The solder should melt and flow into the join. Move your torch to the outside of the ring to draw the solder through the join, and then remove it. Quench, clean, and dry both pieces.

5 Place one ring on the mandrel and tap with the chasing hammer to flatten and enlarge to the desired size. Flip the ring on the mandrel every half size to avoid hammering a taper into the band. Anneal during this process, if necessary. Repeat with the second ring. Both rings should be the exact same size and line up perfectly. If the side edges of the rings are not flush when stacked, then file each ring until they are flush. If further refinement is needed, place the rings one at a time on the bench block and tap with the chasing hammer to even out each edge. Soldering edge to edge is tricky, so you want to make sure you have them as flush and even as possible before you start. If you haven't already, clean both rings.

6 Paint both rings with flux and stack one on top of the other with the seams lined up. Place five small pieces of medium solder on the back quarter of the stack, placing one at the center seam and two more on each side at equal distances apart. The flux should help the solder stick (**fig. 01**).

7 Heat and solder as before, drawing the molten solder through the join with the flame as it flows. One-quarter to one-third of the back section of the ring should now be connected. Pickle and set aside.

NOTE: *If you accidentally solder the whole ring shut, don't panic. Just take your jeweler's saw and gently saw three-quarters of the ring open.*

8 Cut two pieces of 18-gauge fine silver wire at ½" (1.3 cm) and one at ¾" (2 cm). Place these pieces on your kiln brick and heat with the torch until they form two small granules and one larger one.

9 Gently split the edge of your ring opposite the solder by inserting the tip of your chain-nose pliers and opening the jaws carefully. You only want to create a small gap and not break your soldered seam on the other side. Insert a salon board in the opening and file flush.

10 Place the ring on the ring mandrel and use your tweezers to gently press the large granule into the center of the opening. The granule should be held in place by pressure from the sides of the ring and prevented from popping out the back by the ring mandrel. Add the remaining two granules and slide them into place at either end of the opening. Make adjustments as necessary to hold all three granules in place (**fig. 02**).

FIG. 01   FIG. 02

11 Place the ring, granule-side down on your kiln brick. Paint with flux and place easy solder at the seam where each granule meets the band. Solder as above, quench, and clean. Take care not to place too much solder or to overheat, as the granules should retain their shape through this step. The easy solder should flow quite quickly.

12 Oxidize the ring if desired. Remove excess oxidation with fine steel wool.

13 Polish the ring using the brass brush and soap under running water. As an optional finishing step, place the ring in the tumbler and tumble for 45 minutes to work-harden and give a final polish.

TOOLS

PowerMax cutter

Bracelet-bending pliers

Needle files

Permanent marker

Brass-head mallet

Bench block

Chasing hammer

Letter and design stamps (for monogram)

Period stamp or center punch

Screw-down hole punch

Solder setup

Salon board

Medium Wrap n' Tap pliers

Flush cutter

Millimeter gauge

Round-nose pliers

Chain-nose pliers

Bent chain-nose pliers

Sandpaper

Liver of sulfur

Pro Polish pad

MATERIALS

1" (2.5 cm) of 7 × 1 mm sterling silver flat wire (or 20-gauge sterling sheet)

5 pieces of 18-gauge fine silver wire, ⅛" (3 mm) each

Medium and easy paste solder

3" (7.5 mm) of 18-gauge sterling silver wire

12" (30.5 cm) of 16-gauge sterling silver wire

4" (10 cm) of 12-gauge copper wire

¾" (2 cm) of 3 × 1 mm copper flat wire (or cut and hammer out of 12-gauge wire)

1" (2.5 cm) of 14-gauge copper wire

9" (23 cm) of 20-gauge sterling silver wire (for wire wrapping)

Three pearls, 9mm

TECHNIQUES

Sampler square 1, Connecting metal using jump rings

Sampler square 2, Texturing

Sampler square 13, Forming bails

Sampler square 12, Embellishing: Spiral, dots, and granules

monogram chain
BRACELET

This project combines several familiar techniques to make a finished piece of jewelry. The main problem with this one is keeping it all straight, since you make the sections one at a time and don't put it all together until the end. It's really neat to see it come together, though! You might want to keep several dishes handy to keep the components organized, especially if you want to put it away and then work on it later!

 **meet a
new tool**

bracelet-bending pliers

These pliers have nylon jaws that have
a slight bow to bend metal into a cuff
shape perfect for bracelets. They are a
great alternative to the bracelet mandrel,
which is both heavier and more expensive!
Bracelet-bending pliers work on almost
any gauge of soft metal, and the nylon jaws
prevent marring of the metal's surface.

STEPS

MAKE THE MONOGRAM TAG

1 Use your PowerMax cutter to cut your flat
wire to 1" (2.5 cm) in length (or cut a 1"
× ¼" [2.5 × .6 mm] rectangle out of 20 gauge
sheet with a jeweler's saw). File the corners
and place it on your bench block.

2 Stamp it with a monogram and design of
your choice. (I put my last initial in the
middle flanked by dots with the period stamp
and my first and middle initial on either side.)

3 Use your permanent marker to place a
dot about ¹⁄₁₆" (2 mm) in from each end of
this wire and then use the smaller punch on
your screw-down hole punch to make a hole
on each dot. Make two more dots with your
period stamp between these holes and your
monogram. These will position the granules
(**fig. 01**).

4 Grip the tag in the jaws of the bracelet-
bending pliers to give it a slight bow so
it will sit comfortably on your wrist (**fig. 02**).
Set aside.

5 Place the five pieces of fine silver wire on
your kiln brick and heat with the torch
until they melt and form into granules.

6 Place the tag on your kiln brick. Apply
small pieces of medium paste solder to
two of the granules you just made (save the
other three for a later step) and place them
on the dots you just stamped. Turn on your
torch and begin heating. When the binder
has burned away and the piece starts to glow,
move in closer and focus the flame more over

the granules. The solder should flow quickly, adhering your granules to the tag. Quench and clean as always. Set aside.

7 Use the smallest (5 mm) barrel of the medium Wrap n' Tap pliers to make a five-loop coil out of the 18-gauge sterling wire. Use the flush cutter to cut four jump rings from the coil. Remember to flip the cutter with each snip so that the ends of all the jump rings are flush. File if necessary. Set two of these rings aside for a later step.

8 Rotate the other two jump rings to open, then place them through the holes in either end of the tag. Rotate them closed again and make sure they are flush from all angles. Lay the tag on its side in a slot on your kiln brick so the jump rings are flat and the joins are as far from the tag as possible. Place a small amount of easy paste solder on the join of each ring and solder as above. Quench, clean, and file if necessary.

MAKE CHAIN COMPONENTS

9 Use the largest (10 mm) barrel on the medium Wrap n' Tap pliers to make an eight-loop coil from your 16-gauge sterling wire. Use your flush cutters to cut seven rings as above. Set aside.

10 Use the same large barrel of the Wrap n' Tap to make a two-and-a-half-loop coil from the 12-gauge copper wire. Cut two jump rings from the coil with your PowerMax cutter. File the ends flush if necessary. Set aside.

MAKE THE TOGGLE CLASP

11 Begin with a piece of ¾" (2 cm) long copper flat wire or make your own by cutting a ¾" (2 cm) long piece of 12-gauge copper wire and hammering flat on your bench block with a chasing hammer. (The wire may lengthen while flattening, so you may have to trim it back slightly.) Use your period stamp or

center punch to make three evenly spaced dots on one side of this wire.

12 Use your millimeter gauge to find the portion of your round-nose pliers' jaws that are about ⅛" (3 mm) in diameter. Use this portion of the jaws to make a single loop from the 14-gauge copper wire. Use your flush cutter to cut a half-ring bail from this loop. File if necessary.

13 Place the flat wire on your kiln brick with the stamped dots down. Place a small amount of easy paste solder on the ends of the half ring and place it in the center of the wire (**fig. 03**). Use a third hand to hold it if necessary. Solder as above, quench, and clean (**fig. 04**).

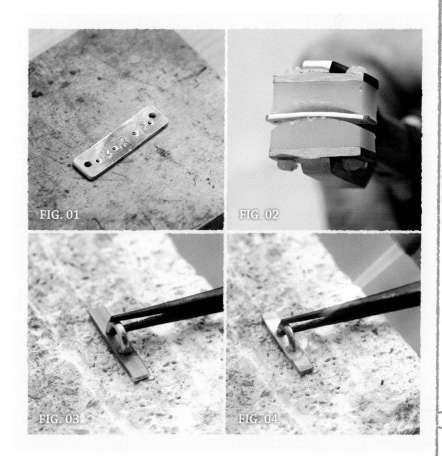

FIG. 01

FIG. 02

FIG. 03

FIG. 04

14 Flip the wire over and place back on the kiln brick with the half loop in a groove so that the flat wire lies flush with the surface of the brick with the stamped dots up. Apply a small amount of easy paste solder to each of the three granules you set aside in step four of "Make the monogram tag" and place them on the stamped dots. Solder as above, quench, and clean.

MAKE THE BRACELET SECTIONS

15 You should now have made: Two 12-gauge copper jump rings, seven 16-gauge silver jump rings, two small 18-gauge jump rings, the toggle bar, and the monogram tag with attached jump rings.

16 Link one of the small 18-gauge silver jump rings through the half-ring bail on the toggle bar. Solder using easy paste solder and set aside.

17 Link two of the 16-gauge silver jump rings together and solder both joins with easy solder. Hammer flat with your chasing hammer and set aside.

18 Solder both of the 12-gauge copper jump rings closed. Hammer flat. Set aside.

19 Open one of the remaining 16-gauge silver jump rings and thread it first through the jump ring on the left side of the monogram tag and then through one of the 12-gauge copper jump rings. Solder closed, quench, clean, dry, and hammer flat.

20 On the other side of the mono-grammed tag, attach four of the 16-gauge rings. Attach each one separately. Solder, quench, clean, dry, and flatten each ring before attaching the next one

21 Solder the final small 18-gauge jump ring to the remaining 12-gauge copper ring.

22 You should now be able to lay out the four sections of the bracelet as shown here (**fig. 05**).

ASSEMBLE THE BRACELET

23 Wire wrap the first pearl (see page 157) so that one loop goes through the jump ring attached to the toggle bar and the other through one of the jump rings in the two-ring section of the chain.

24 Wire wrap the next pearl so that one loop attaches to the two-ring section of chain and the other to the large copper ring at one end of the section with the monogram tag.

25 Wire wrap the final pearl so that one end loop attaches to the end of the monogram tag section and the other goes through the small loop in the final section.

26 Oxidize using liver of sulfur and polish with a Pro Polish pad.

FIG. 05

wrapped toggle CLASP

This is a great way to jazz up the basic toggle clasp. The clean lines and texture are perfectly understated, adding interest to your jewelry but not stealing anybody's thunder. If you want, you can add or remove jump rings to adjust the length.

STEPS

MAKE THE TOGGLE BAR

1 Use your ruler and permanent marker to mark your rivet tube at 1" (2.5 cm). Grip in the tube-cutting pliers so the mark lines up with the slot in the jaws and cut with the jeweler's saw. File the ends flush with your salon board.

2 Measure to find the midpoint of the tube and mark with your marker. Grip again in the tube-cutting pliers and make a cut partway through, just enough to make a small opening in one tube wall. This opening will vent the heat when you set the granules (**fig. 01**). Set aside.

3 Place the two pieces of 12-gauge fine silver wire on your kiln brick and melt into granules. Allow to air cool.

4 Apply hard paste solder to the inside rim of each end of the tube and place the tube on your kiln brick. Push the granules into each end of the tube gently. They should be held in place by the paste solder (**fig. 02**).

5 Turn on your torch and begin heating. When the binder has burned away and the pieces start to glow, move in closer and focus the flame more over the tube ends. The solder should flow and hold the granules in place. Remove your torch, quench, and clean both pieces. Be careful not to overheat because that will melt the granules.

6 Use the bead wire to make a three-loop coil around the tube. Cut with your flush cutter. Place small pieces of solder around the middle of your tube. Slide the coil onto the tube and solder in place as above. The coil should cover the opening you made earlier to vent the heat (**fig. 03**).

7 Use your millimeter gauge to find the portion of the jaw on your round-nose pliers that is four millimeters in diameter. Mark with your permanent marker at this point and make a five-loop coil out of your 16-gauge sterling wire.

8 Cut three full rings and one half ring off this coil, flipping the cutters with each clip to make sure the ends of all the rings are flush.

9 Lay your wrapped tube on its side in a shallow groove in your kiln brick so that when you lay the half ring on the surface of the brick, the ends are centered on the tube (**fig. 04**). Apply easy paste solder to the ends of the half ring and solder as above.

10 Link one of the full rings through the bail you just made so that the join is

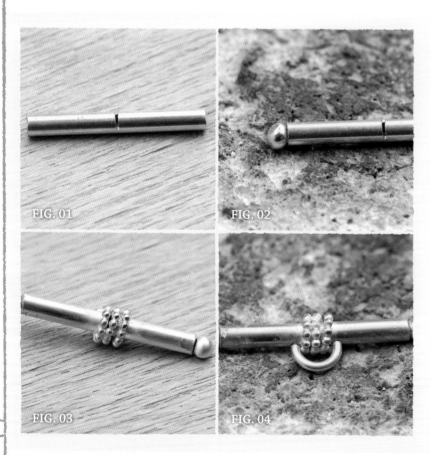

FIG. 01

FIG. 02

FIG. 03

FIG. 04

as far from the bar as possible. Apply a small amount of easy paste solder to the join and solder as above. Repeat with the next two rings so that you have a chain of three rings on the bail (**fig. 05**). Quench, clean, and file away any excess solder.

MAKE THE TOGGLE LOOP

11 Anneal your 10-gauge sterling wire, then use the small (13 mm) barrel of your large Wrap n' Tap pliers to make a loop out of it. Cut with your PowerMax cutter, keeping both ends of the ring flush. File if necessary.

12 Use your chain-nose and bent chain-nose pliers to make sure the ends of the ring line up in all directions to form a flush join. Place the ring on your kiln brick and solder with hard paste solder as above. Quench and clean as always.

13 Place the ring on your bench block and tap it with the plastic mallet to make sure it is completely level.

14 Use the bead wire as above to wrap a three-loop coil around the ring. Cut and solder in place with medium solder just as you did on the toggle bar.

15 Make a loop for the bail out of the bead wire on the 4mm portion of your round-nose pliers as you did before. Cut a half ring using the flush cutters as before.

16 Lay your toggle loop flat on your kiln brick. Apply a small amount of easy paste solder to the ends of the bail and lay it on the surface of the brick so the ends of the bail are touching the ring (**fig. 06**).

17 Solder as above, quench, and clean.

18 Make another jump ring out of the bead wire on the round-nose pliers. (I made this one slightly larger.) Place it

FIG. 05

FIG. 06

FIG. 07

through the bail on the loop and solder with easy paste solder as before (**fig. 07**).

19 Oxidize the entire clasp with liver of sulfur, if desired, and polish.

TOOLS

Ring mandrel
PowerMax flush cutter
Large Wrap n' Tap
  pliers
Bench block
Chasing hammer
Plastic mallet
Equaling file
Fine-grit sandpaper
Solder setup / Max
  Flame torch
Jeweler's saw and cut
  lubricant
Bench pin
Needle files
Slash design stamp
Period design stamp
Round-nose pliers
Scissors (for cutting out
  flower template)
Fine-tip permanent
  marker
Divider
Chain-nose pliers
Third hand
Half-round file
Liver of sulfur
Burnisher

MATERIALS

5 mm × 1 mm flat wire
  (Amount determined
  by the size of the
  band.)
Rubber cement
1" (2.5 cm) diameter
  22-gauge sterling
  silver circle or a piece
  of 22-gauge sterling
  sheet at least 1" × 1"
  (2.5 × 2.5 cm)
⅛" (3 mm) wide fine
  silver scalloped bezel
  wire
11 × 9 mm oval
  cabochon stone
Painter's tape
Hard and medium wire
  or sheet solder
Easy paste solder
Flux and brush
Dental floss

TECHNIQUES

Sampler square 2,
  Texturing
Sampler square 5,
  Work-hardening,
  annealing, and
  cleaning fire scale
Sampler square 10,
  Sawing and soldering
  a cut shape
Sampler square 11,
  Two-step soldering
Sampler square 15,
  Making a bezel and
  setting a stone

flower
RING

This simple design is perfect for showcasing a special cabochon stone. If you prefer to enhance the design with more texture and stamping, take the idea and run with it! I used scalloped bezel wire for this design. The technique is the same as with regular bezel wire, except the tips of the scallops curve in to hold the stone in place instead of the entire rim of the bezel.

meet a new tool

equaling file

This file is flat and has a filing surface on both sides. This is the file to use when you are trying to make two sides of metal fit flush together such as the ends of a ring band.

STEPS

MAKING THE BAND

1 Use the Max Flame torch for this project if you have one. Cut a strip of paper ¼" (6 mm) wide by 4" (10 cm) long. Choose the finger that the ring should fit on and wrap the strip of paper around the knuckle of that finger. (Since the knuckle is the largest part of

the finger, the ring will have to slide over the knuckle to fit.) Mark the measurement. Use the millimeter gauge to measure the thickness of the gauge of metal (usually about 1 mm or so.) Measure the length of paper that went around your finger in millimeters and add the thickness of the metal to that number. This number is the length to cut your metal strip for the ring band. Cut the flat wire to the correct length using the PowerMax flush cutter.

2 Check that both cut ends of the wire are flush. Anneal the wire and use the center barrel of the large Wrap n' Tap pliers (16 mm) to shape the strip into a circle. Don't worry about shaping it into a perfect ring at this time, as it will be perfected after soldering. Anneal again if the metal stiffens up while you are shaping it. Remember there is no need to clean the ring until after the final annealing step.

3 With your fingers, push the ends of the ring together so that they are closed flush against each other. Refine the join, still using your fingers, by pushing one end of the band up and over the other and then pull back into place. The edges should "pop" together and form a flush join. If it is not quite flush, repeat this step with the opposite end. Check to make sure that the join is even all the way around. File with the equaling file or a folded piece of fine-grit sandpaper to refine the join if needed (**fig. 01**).

4 Place the ring on the kiln brick with the join facing away from you. Apply flux and hard solder to the seam on the inside of the band. Turn on your torch and begin heating. When the flux becomes glassy and the pieces start to glow, move in closer and focus the flame more over the solder. The solder should melt and flow into the join. As the solder flows, move the torch flame to the outside of the join to draw the solder through the seam. Remove your torch, quench, and clean the band.

FIG. 01

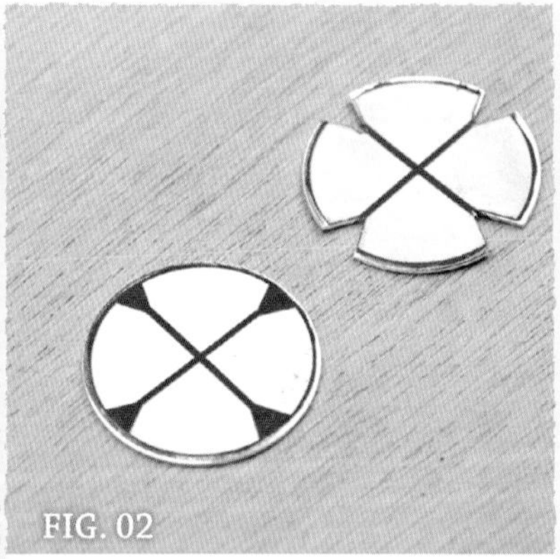

FIG. 02

FIG. 03

FIG. 04

5 Now is the time to get that ring nice and round. Slide the ring on a ring mandrel and tap into shape using the plastic mallet. Flip the ring and tap again so the ring is not hammered into a tapered shape. If the ring is round but is a bit warped, place it flat on a bench block and tap with the mallet. Flip and tap again. This should true up the shape. (Don't worry about filing the seam in the band at this time.)

MAKE THE BEZEL SETTING

6 Trace or photocopy the flower pattern on page 155 onto a piece of plain white paper. Cut out the template with scissors and use rubber cement to glue it to the 1" (2.5 cm) diameter 22-gauge blank. The edges of the pattern should line up with the edges of the blank. Let the rubber cement dry so the pattern is firmly adhered to the metal.

7 Use a jeweler's saw to saw along the lines of the V-shaped notches on the pattern. Remember to anchor your blade in the wood of the bench pin to begin your cut. (See **fig. 02** for pre- and post-cut.)

8 After the design is cut out, peel the paper off of the metal. File the edges of the flower smooth. If you are using sheet metal instead of a pre-made blank, you'll have to cut out the entire piece instead of just the notches.

9 Place the cabochon stone on the center of the bezel back that you just made and use a fine-tipped permanent marker to trace around the stone (**fig. 03**). You can use stamps to texture the flowers around the stone. I used the period stamp flanked by a slash stamp on either side. Slightly round the edges of each petal with your round-nose pliers after stamping.

NOTE: *If you have trouble with the stone slipping as you trace it, put a dot of rubber cement down to hold the stone in place. You can easily pop the stone up when you are done.*

10 Measure and cut a piece of bezel wire to fit the stone using the painter's tape trick (see page 71). I try and cut the wire so that the scallops line up correctly. If I have to make the bezel just a bit too small to get them to line up, then I can enlarge the bezel by taping it on a ring mandrel with a rubber mallet. Solder the bezel closed using hard solder. Quench and clean. Fit your stone into the soldered bezel to check the fit.

NOTE: *If you have to cut the width of the bezel wire for a smaller stone, you will need to subtract the desired width from the total width of the wire. You will measure from the flat edge because you can't use the divider with a scalloped edge.*

11 Solder the bezel to the flower with medium solder. Quench and clean.

12 Check the solder join all around to make sure that the bezel is completely soldered to the flower. If there are gaps, lightly tap them flush with a plastic mallet to close and re-solder.

13 Place the flower bezel-side down on your kiln brick. Apply easy paste solder to the back of the flower. Use the third hand to position the band with the seam down against the flower (**fig. 04**). Solder, quench, and clean the ring.

14 File away the seam on the inside of the ring using the half-round file. Follow up by using fine-grit sandpaper to smooth out any marks left by the file.

15 Oxidize the ring, dry, and polish using a Pro Polish pad, brass brush, or tumbler.

16 Set the stone in the bezel. Remember to test it with dental floss first! Burnish the sides of the bezel over the edges of the stone to hold the stone in place.

TOOLS

Jeweler's ruler
PowerMax flush cutter
Medium Wrap n' Tap pliers
Flush cutter
Chasing hammer
Bench block
Screw-down hole punch
Solder setup
Third hand
Large Wrap n' Tap pliers
Sandpaper
Round-nose pliers
Chain-nose pliers
Bent chain-nose pliers
Liver of sulfur
Pro Polish pads
File

MATERIALS

5 × 1 mm sterling silver flat wire, 1" (2.5 cm)
16-gauge sterling silver wire, 5" (12.5 cm)
Small scrap of sterling silver sheet, 24-gauge (for punching dots out of)
14-gauge sterling silver wire, 4" (10 cm)
24-gauge sterling silver wire, 6" (15 cm)
Hard, medium, and easy paste solder
Assortment of 4mm beads

TECHNIQUES

Sampler square 1, Connecting metal using jump rings
Sampler square 4, Riveting
Sampler square 12, Embellishing: Spiral, dots, and granules
Sampler square 13, Forming bails

dangly
TOGGLE

This is a great piece to add some flair to a necklace or bracelet. Be sure to make the toggle bar first, as the size of the ring for the clasp depends on the size of the bar. Embellish with beads of your choice from any color palette!

STEPS

MAKE THE TOGGLE BAR

1 Cut 1" (2.5 cm) of 5 mm flat wire. File each end of the wire so that they are slightly rounded.

2 Using 16-gauge wire, make a four-wrap coil using the smallest barrel (5 mm) on the medium Wrap n' Tap pliers. Use a flush cutter to cut four half rings (bails) from the coil. Flatten each half ring with the chasing hammer on a bench block. File the ends flush if needed and set aside.

3 Use the large (2.3 mm) side of the screw-down hole punch to punch three dots from the scrap of 24-gauge sheet.

4 Apply small amounts of hard solder to two of these dots and place one dot near the edge on one end of your flat wire. Place hard solder on the ends of the bail and place it down on the bar next to the dot. Apply hard solder to the second dot and place it on the flat wire, on the other side of the bail in the center. Be sure to leave enough room for another half ring and final dot. Secure the half ring in place with your third hand (**fig. 01**).

5 Turn on your torch and begin heating. When the binder has burned away and the pieces start to glow, move in closer and focus the flame more over the solder. The solder should melt and flow and the pieces should settle. Remove your torch, quench, and clean.

6 Place the second half ring and the last dot on the toggle bar and solder as before with medium paste solder. Quench and clean.

7 Carve a slight depression into the kiln brick and set the toggle into it smooth-side up. Solder a third half ring to the center of this side with easy solder (**fig. 02**). Clean and set aside.

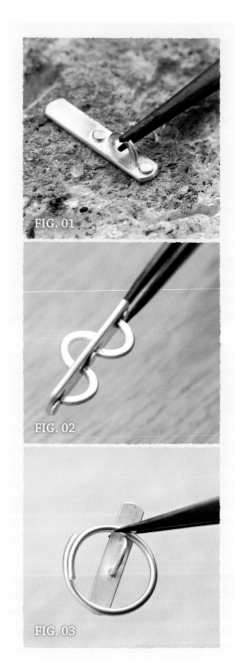

FIG. 01

FIG. 02

FIG. 03

MAKE THE LOOP

8 Using 14-gauge wire, make a single loop around the center barrel (16mm) of the large Wrap n' Tap pliers. The ends of the wire should slightly overlap to allow for sizing. Before cutting, lay the toggle bar on the loop with the single half-ring side down. Slide the bar so this half ring is touching one side of the loop. If the end of the bar is still lying on the loop, then it will be a secure toggle—the loop will not slip through. It is important to size the loop before cutting so your clasp will be effective as well as beautiful (**fig. 03**). If your toggle is smaller than the loop, then the loop is too large. Use your fingers to bend it tighter before cutting the ends.

9 Cut the ends of the loop flush with the PowerMax flush cutter. Solder with hard solder and clean as above. Flatten the loop using the chasing hammer and bench block.

FIG. 04

FIG. 05

Texture both sides of the loop with the ball end of the chasing hammer.

10 Use the large (2.3 mm) side of the screw-down hole punch to punch four more dots from the scrap of 24-gauge sheet.

11 File the ends of the last half ring to a slight diagonal so that the ring fits flush with the edge of the bottom of the loop. Lay the loop flat on your soldering surface. Place two dots on top of the loop on opposing sides and the half ring next to the loop with the ends touching, centered on one of the dots (**fig. 04**). Solder the half ring and dots at the same time with medium solder as above and clean.

12 Flip the loop over and solder two more dots at the top and bottom center on the loop. Solder with easy solder, then clean.

13 Oxidize and polish both pieces of the clasp and set aside.

MAKE THE BEAD EMBELLISHMENT

14 Cut the 24-gauge wire into six 1" (2.5 cm) pieces. Make six balled head pins by holding each wire in your tweezers at a slight angle and directing your torch flame at the lower quarter from the side. When the wire starts to glow, move the angle of the torch to focus the sweet spot of the flame directly at the end of the wire. When the ball forms, flick the flame up the wire and then remove it. Quench and clean. For more detailed instructions, see sampler square 4 (see page 44). Oxidize the finished head pins.

15 Place one bead on each head pin. Use the round- and chain-nose pliers to wire wrap three dangles to each half loop on the toggle bar (**fig. 05**). (See page 157 for how to wire wrap.)

TOOLS

Permanent marker
Jeweler's saw and cut
    lubricant
Bench pin
Needle files
Salon board
Ruler
Permanent marker
Center punch or
    period stamp
Letter stamp set
Screw-down hole
    punch
Tube-cutting pliers
Power-punch pliers
Brass-head mallet
Rivet hammer or other
    texture hammer
Solder setup / Max
    Flame torch
Liver of sulfur
Pro Polish pad

MATERIALS

3" × 2" (7.5 × 5 cm)
    of 22-gauge nickel
    silver sheet
1/8" diameter brass
    rivet tube
Four pieces of 16-gauge
    fine silver wire, 1/2"
    (1.3 cm) each

22-gauge sterling
    silver wire, 3"
    (7.5 cm)
3/4" (2 cm) brass circle
    blank, 24-gauge
Hard and medium wire
    or sheet solder
Easy paste solder
1" (2.5 cm) round
    mirror
One 10mm freshwater
    pearl
1/8" (3 mm) scalloped
    fine silver bezel wire
Painter's tape

TECHNIQUES

Sampler square 1,
    Connecting metal
    using jump rings
Sampler square 2,
    Texturing
Sampler square 4,
    Riveting
Sampler square
    10, Sawing and
    soldering a cut
    shape
Sampler square 15,
    Making a bezel and
    setting a stone

mirror
PENDANT

This pretty pendant features a mirror in the setting. The mirror can be replaced with a stone or just a simple texture or soldered design. Cleaning this piece and removing the fire scale may be a bit more challenging because of the high amount of heat needed to solder this piece. Try buffing the pieces using fine-grit sandpaper or sanding sponges. This gives the piece a nice matte finish and helps to remove any stubborn dark spots or copper residue. Since this piece is large, the Max Flame torch is best used with this project.

STEPS

1 Trace or photocopy the mirror template from page 155. Use rubber cement to apply the template to your nickel sheet. Saw out the shape using your jeweler's saw. Remember to stabilize the saw in the bench pin before beginning your cut. After the design is cut out, peel the paper off of the metal. File the edges of the shape smooth. For added interest, use the tapered end of the riveting hammer to tap close-set lines around the edge of one side of the mirror shape.

2 Stamp four equally spaced dots using the period stamp or center punch around the circle section of the mirror shape on the textured side. (These will be used for placement of the granules to be soldered on later.)

3 Use the ⅛" (3mm) hole punch in the power-punch pliers to make a hole at the top of the handle part of the mirror cutout. Set the piece aside.

4 Use your ruler and permanent marker to mark your rivet tube at ⅟₁₆" (2 mm). Grip in the tube-cutting pliers so the mark lines up with the slot in the jaws, then cut with the jeweler's saw. Rivet the tube in place in the hole in the handle of the mirror shape.

5 Place the four pieces of 16-gauge fine silver wire on your kiln brick and melt them into granules. Set aside.

6 Stamp the ¾" (2 cm) brass blank with your name, initials, or a pattern of your choice. Set this stamped piece aside.

7 Measure and cut a piece of bezel wire to fit the 1" (2.5 cm) mirror using the painter's tape trick (see page 71). Solder the bezel closed using hard solder. Pickle. Fit your mirror into the soldered bezel to check the fit.

8 Solder the bezel to the side of the mirror shape that has no hammer texture, using medium solder (**fig. 01**). Quench and clean.

9 Check the solder join all around to make sure that the bezel is completely soldered to the shape. If there are gaps, lightly tap them flush with a plastic mallet to close and resolder.

10 Flip the mirror shape over so that the textured side is facing up and the bezel is facing down. Place and solder the stamped brass circle and granules using easy paste solder. Quench and clean.

11 Oxidize the piece using liver of sulfur and polish with a Pro Polish pad.

12 Set the mirror in the bezel. Remember to test it with dental floss first! Burnish the sides of the bezel over the edges of the mirror to hold mirror in place (**fig. 02**).

13 As a final embellishment, use 22-gauge wire to wire wrap a pearl into the hole in the mirror handle, where the pendant may be hung. (See page 157 for wire wrapping.)

FIG. 01

FIG. 02

pearl
tablet
CLASP

A clasp can be equally at home in the front of a necklace as well as at the back, especially when it is as decorative as this one. It would look lovely offset slightly to the side of a finished strand of pearls or other simple beads, letting the clasp be the focus of the design.

TOOLS
Divider
Bench block
Plastic mallet
Salon board
Round-nose pliers
Medium Wrap n' Tap pliers
Flush cutter
French shears
Chain-nose pliers
Millimeter gauge
Solder setup
Disc cutter (optional)
Chasing hammer
Power-punch pliers
Dapping block
Brass-head mallet
Riveting hammer
Liver of sulfur

MATERIALS
24-gauge sterling silver sheet
16-gauge sterling silver wire, 4" (10 cm)
One circle of 24-gauge sterling silver, ¾" (2 cm) (or cut your own with a disc cutter)
One circle of 24-gauge sterling sheet, ⁹⁄₃₂" (7 mm) (I punched my own with power-punch pliers.)
½" (1.3 cm) of 16-gauge fine silver wire
One long sterling silver head pin, 24-gauge, 1" (2.5 cm) (use pre-made or make your own)
One freshwater pearl, 4mm
Paste solder, easy, medium, and hard

TECHNIQUES
Sampler square 4, Riveting
Sampler square 10, Sawing and soldering a cut shape
Sampler square 12 Embellishing: Spiral, dots, and granules
Sampler square 13, Forming bails
Sampler square 14, Shaping and soldering domes

STEPS

MAKE THE HOOK

1 Set the tips of the divider at ⅛" (3mm) apart and use it to mark a strip on 24-gauge sterling sheet. Cut this strip to 1½" (3.8 cm) long using the French shears. Place the strip on a bench block and flatten with the plastic mallet.

2 Use a salon board to file the edges smooth and round the corners of one narrow end of the strip. This is the end that will be formed into the hook. The other end should be filed square.

3 Use the round-nose pliers to form a small loop on the square end of the strip. Use the chain-nose pliers, if needed, to make the edge of the loop sit tightly against the hook (**fig. 01**). Remember to anneal if the metal becomes too hard to work and file if necessary.

4 Place the hook on your kiln brick so the join in the loop is up. Apply a small amount of easy paste solder to the loop join. Turn on your torch and begin heating. When the binder has burned away and the piece starts to glow, move in closer and focus the flame more over the solder. The solder should melt and flow into the join. Remove your torch, quench, and clean.

5 Use a millimeter gauge to determine the ³⁄₁₆" (5 mm) measurement on the barrel of the round-nose pliers. (You can use your permanent marker to mark this point on your pliers.) Use the round-nose pliers to grip the strip about ⅝" (1.5 cm) from the unsoldered end and bend the strip around the barrel to form the hook shape (**fig. 02**). Grip the tip of the hook with your chain-nose pliers and bend slightly to flare out.

6 Use the smallest (5mm) barrel of the Wrap n' Tap pliers to make the 18-gauge wire into a coil for jump rings. Cut three rings from the coil using the flush cutter. Remember to flip the cutter with each clip to make sure the ends of all the rings are flat.

7 Rotate one jump ring open and put it through the loop in the hook. Place it on your kiln brick so the join is as far from the hook as possible. Solder it closed with easy paste solder as above. Quench, clean, dry, and then tap the ring flat on the edge of your bench block with the chasing hammer. Rotate as you tap to flatten all the way around.

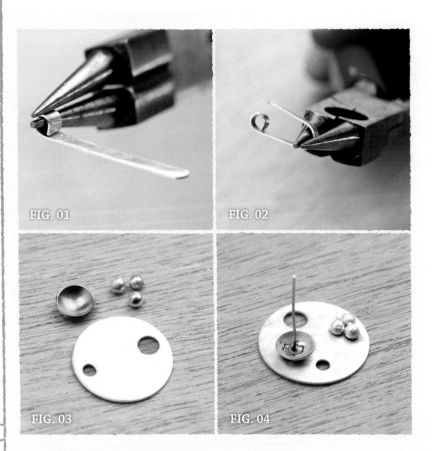

FIG. 01

FIG. 02

FIG. 03

FIG. 04

8 Add another ring to the one you just finished, using the same method. Rotate it open. Put it through the first ring with the seam as far away as possible. Solder with easy paste solder. Quench, clean, dry, and flatten as above.

MAKE THE TABLET

9 Select a pre-made ¾" (2 cm) disc or cut one from 24-gauge sheet with a disc cutter. Use the power-punch pliers to make a ³⁄₃₂" (2.4 mm) hole 2mm in from the edge of the disc. Punch a ⁵⁄₃₂" (4 mm) hole 2 mm in from the opposite edge. Set aside.

10 Use the power-punch pliers to cut a ⁹⁄₃₂" (7 mm) disc from 24-gauge sterling silver then dap it into a dome using the metal dapping block.

11 Cut the 16-gauge fine silver wire into three ¼" (6 mm) pieces. Place them on your kiln brick and heat them until they form granules (**fig. 03**).

12 Place the ¾" (2 cm) disc on your soldering surface with the small hole toward you and the large hole away from you. Add hard paste solder to the back of each granule and arrange them in a triangular pattern on the right side of the disc starting at about ¹⁄₁₆" (2 mm) from the edge. Solder as above, quench, and clean.

13 Return the disc to the soldering surface. Add medium paste solder to the bottom of the dapped dome. Place it edge up on the left-hand side of the disc, opposite the granules. Solder as above, quench, and clean.

THE TABLET PART OF THE CLASP WOULD ALSO MAKE A NICE CENTERPIECE FOR A RING.

14 Return the disc to the soldering surface one last time. Grip the head pin in the soldering tweezers and set them aside so they are ready. Place easy solder in the bottom of the dome and heat with the torch. As the solder melts, place the ball end of the pin in the center of the dome. Quickly remove the torch. The head pin should now be soldered in the center of the dome (**fig. 04**). Quench and clean.

15 Cut a jump ring from the coil that you set aside earlier. Place it through the ³⁄₃₂" (2.4 mm) hole in the disc and solder closed with easy paste solder. Quench, clean, and dry.

16 Place the ring on the edge of a bench block and flatten using a chasing hammer as you did for the rings on the hook.

17 Slide a pearl onto the headpin so it sits down in the cup. Cut away excess wire leaving a scant ¹⁄₁₆" (2 mm) above the hole. Use a riveting hammer to rivet the pearl in place.

18 Oxidize with both the hook and tablet sides of the clasp with liver of sulfur and polish with a Pro Polish pad.

acknowledgments

Writing this book was a labor of love. Teaching is my passion, and sharing my knowledge between the covers of a book is a dream come true. I feel like this is my Academy Awards speech, so I'd better get on with it before the music plays me off stage.

First and foremost I would like to thank Kris Gucker. He helped me refine my writing voice and worked tirelessly on editing, reviewing, and organizing this material. Without his help, this book would not exist.

To my tester team. Beth Colbert, Zoe Ferrant, Jessica Gaston, Diane Owens, Karen Monique Chan, Winnie van der Rijn, Liz Gucker, Susan Cole, Mark, Mary, and Katie Cravens—thank you for cutting, sawing, filing, and soldering. The testing sessions made the book so much better. I thank you and I'll bet the readers will, too.

A big thanks goes out to the team at Interweave, and especially to my editor, Erica Smith. You are amazing. Thanks for helping to keep it all together.

To Mary Cravens, my stylist in all things. Thanks for lending your artistic eye to this project. Your taste is impeccable. I owe you a dry martini.

To my mom, Guin Jenanyan. You are always my biggest cheerleader. Thanks for your encouragement and unwavering confidence that I can do whatever I put my mind to. You are the craftiest person I know! I lovingly dedicate this book to you.

TEMPLATES

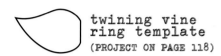
twining vine
ring template
(PROJECT ON PAGE 118)

flower ring
template
(PROJECT ON PAGE 140)

mirror
pendant
template
(PROJECT
ON PAGE 148)

soldered
key pendant
template
(PROJECT ON PAGE 109)

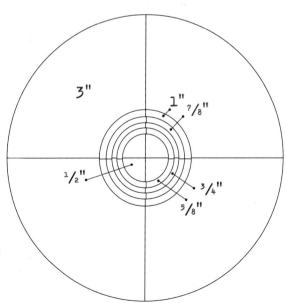

circle center
finder

JUST PLACE YOUR BLANK
IN THE CIRCLE OF THE
APPROPRIATE SIZE AND
THEN USE YOUR STRAIGHT
EDGE AND MARKER TO
COMPLETE THE STRAIGHT
LINES. WHERE THEY CROSS
IS THE CENTER OF YOUR
BLANK.

3"

1"

7/8"

1/2"

3/4"

5/8"

TECHNIQUES

SIMPLE LOOP

To form a simple loop, use flat-nose pliers to make a 90-degree bend at least ½" (1.3 cm) from the end of the wire. Use round-nose pliers to grasp the wire after the bend; roll the pliers toward the bend, but not past it, to preserve the 90-degree bend. Use your thumb to continue the wrap around the nose of the pliers. Trim the wire next to the bend. Open a simple loop just as you would a jump ring.

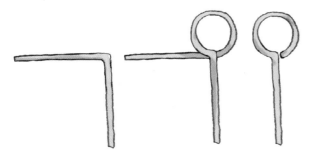

WRAPPED LOOP

To form a wrapped loop, begin with a 90-degree bend at least 2" (5 cm) from the end of the wire. Use round-nose pliers to form a simple loop with a tail overlapping the bend. Wrap the tail tightly down the neck of the wire to create a couple of coils. Trim the excess wire to finish. Make a double-wrapped loop by wrapping the wire back up over the coils, toward the loop, and trimming the wire tail at the loop.

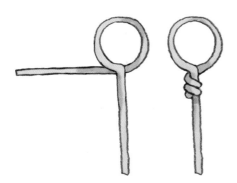

WRAPPED-LOOP DANGLES

Dangles can be strung as they are, attached using jump rings, or linked to other loops. Use a head pin or eye pin to string the bead(s), then form a simple or wrapped loop.

WRAPPED-LOOP LINKS

Link a wrapped loop to another loop by passing the wire through the previous loop before wrapping the tail down the neck of the wire.

WRAPPED-LOOP BAILS

Wrapped-loop bails turn side-drilled beads, usually teardrops, into pendants. Center the bead on a 3" (7.5 cm) or longer piece of wire. Bend both ends of the wire up the sides and across the to of the bead. Bend one end straight up at the center of the dead, then wrap the other wire around it to form a couple of coils. Form a wrapped loop with the straight-up wire, wrapping it back down over the already-formed coils. Trim the excess wire.

RESOURCES

GENERAL METALWORKING SUPPLIES

Beaducation
(650) 261-1870
beaducation.com

Kate Richbourg Jewelry
etsy.com/shop/KateRichbourgJewelry

Rio Grande
(800) 545-6566
riogrande.com

Otto Frei
ottofrei.com

HANDCUT CABOCHONS

Gary Wilson Stones
garywilsonstones.com

Lost Sierra
etsy.com/shop/LostSierra

COPPER AND BRASS WIRE AND BEZELS

Just Wire
etsy.com/shop/JustWire

INDEX

get fired up ABOUT THESE OTHER HOT
JEWELRY-MAKING RESOURCES FROM INTERWEAVE

THE WORKBENCH G
TO JEWELRY TECHN

Anastasia Young

ISBN 978-1-59668-16

$34.95

**SILVERSMITHING FOR
JEWELRY MAKERS**

A Handbook of Techniques
and Surface Treatments

Elizabeth Bone

ISBN 978-1-59668-499-7

$30.00

 Bead...

...lry Making Daily

Whether you've just started
there's a place for you at Be
online community. A free e-
projects, a daily blog, tips a
announcements, event new
are just some of the treats
beadingdaily.com.

...y is the ultimate online
...one interested in creating
Get tips from industry experts,
...-by-step projects, check out
...ver sources for supplies, and
...welrymakingdaily.com.